the Bible
Reading
REVOLUTION

An Easy Guide to Bible Reading

By

Ellen Johnson Varughese

The Bible Reading Revolution
An Easy Guide to Bible Reading

Unless otherwise noted, Scripture is taken from the New King James Version. Copyright © 1982 by Thomas Nelson, Inc. Used by permission. All rights reserved.

Scripture quotations marked ESV are from the ESV® Bible (The Holy Bible, English Standard Version®), copyright © 2001 by Crossway, a publishing ministry of Good News Publishers. Used by permission. All rights reserved.

Scripture quotations marked NASB are taken from the NEW AMERICAN STANDARD BIBLE®, Copyright © 1960,1962,1963,1968,1 971,1972,1973,1975,1977,1995 by The Lockman Foundation. Used by permission.

Scripture quotations marked KJV are taken from the King James Version of the Bible.

ISBN: 978-0-9632670-1-6
Library of Congress Control Number: 2019916370

First printing: 2019
Printed in the USA

JoyPress
P.O. Box 3025
Olathe, KS   66063

website: www.biblerr.com

The Bible Reader's Creed

*With God's help, I will read my Bible
every word, in the proportion that God gave
over and over again for the rest of my life.*

Table of Contents

Introduction

When the Lord called me to write this book some years ago, I was struck by the thought of what a revolution there would be in our Christian community if all of us suddenly started reading our Bibles consistently and with a passion for knowing God.

As you'll read in Chapter 1, I was a devoted Christian who had somehow missed the message that if I wanted to know God, it would be a good idea to read the Bible, every word of it.

Yes, I went to Bible studies (lots of them) when I was in college. We'd get together and decide we wanted to study, say, Ephesians. So we would pick the book apart, verse by verse, and maybe we'd learn something. But somehow, we missed the part about understanding what the central message of the book was.

Eventually, I figured out that the first step in studying Ephesians is, strangely enough, to *read the book!* We need to read it several times to gain a strong overview of what Paul wanted the people of Ephesus to understand. Then, and only then, are we in a position to examine it deeply, verse by verse.

What a revolutionary thought! Read the book before you pick it apart! It follows, then, that to understand any portion of the Bible, we must *read the Bible!*

Could we ever hope to understand Ephesians without understanding the entire counsel of God?

No, we must read our Bibles.

In my way of thinking, to draw genuinely know God and to draw close to Him we must do three things: *read* the Bible, *study* the Bible, and *obey* the Bible. When we saturate our minds and our entire lifestyle with these three elements, we will be transformed into children after

God's own heart.

I have entitled this book *The Bible Reading Revolution* because I long for the revolutionary transformation I am talking about.

The revolution will occur at three levels. First, the Word of God will transform us individually as we read, study and obey His instructions for our daily lives.

Second, if our churches get serious about reading, studying, and obeying the Bible, we will start a revolution in within our church walls.

Lastly, our obedience to the Lord will spill out into the greater society. I would like to see a revolution in America (and the world for that matter) that produces revivals such as the great Welsh revival in the beginning of the 20th century.

This is a book about Bible reading. I'm a tremendous fan of serious Bible study, but I consider that a different discipline with its own set of techniques. The first step toward Bible study is to read the Bible, every word of it.

We'll see this repeatedly in this book, but here is the Bible Reader's Creed:

With God's help, I will read my Bible,
every word, in the proportion that God gave,
over and over again for the rest of my life.

How to Use this Book

I grew up near the ocean in California. From the time I can remember, my brother and sister and I would splash in the waves at Gaviota Beach. Sometimes we would wade out to chest-deep water, always a thrilling experience.

I associate this surface activity to Bible reading. Aside from a few boat rides, I have never explored the Pacific Ocean from beyond chest deep water.

If I ever got the urge to study the entire Pacific Ocean, I might get a PhD in Oceanography, and I might try to find the most state-of-the-art boat and the most modern exploring equipment. Still, I wouldn't get very far. The Pacific Ocean is simply too *huge*. Likewise, all my attempts at serious Bible study have shown me that I'm still just skimming the surface. The Word of God is deep, very deep.

This is a book about Bible reading. It is not a book about Bible study, which I believe to be a separate discipline. In this book we are enjoying the tide pools and breakers along the shoreline. That said, we are reading with a purpose. We want to learn everything we can from the surface view, and we want to draw closer to the Lord.

If you are new to the Word of God, I've kept you in mind. I'll guide you through your first baby steps as you splash around. If you've been a Christian for a while, I'll do my best to take you to chest-deep. Anything beyond that comes under the category of Bible study.

Part I is my introduction to Bible reading. I tell my experience and I explain the difference between Bible reading and Bible study.

Part II tells a few things about Bible basics, how it's set up, it's central message, its various book classifications and so forth.

Part III is my "How to Read" series. Reading a book of poetry is quite different from reading a book of prophecy. You'll get a few tips in this section.

Part IV is where I introduce each book of the Bible. My descriptions are short, just tiny springboards to get you oriented before you start reading.

This book is intended to be a handbook, a simple guide, so please don't spend too much time reading it.

Read your Bible!

Part I

The Challenge of Bible Reading

Chapter 1

Beauty Beyond Description

In California, where I come from, we have the magnificent Sequoia trees, the largest trees on earth. When I was a student at Fresno State University, friends and I would sometimes head for Yosemite National Park on free afternoons. On our way to the valley with its waterfalls, we would stop off at the Mariposa Grove, a quiet, serene grove of *Sequoiadenderon Gigantea*, most of them over two hundred feet tall and thirty feet in diameter at the base. I never wanted to go straight to the valley. The Mariposa Grove must never be passed by in my opinion.

There are several groves of Giant Sequoias in the Sierra Nevada Mountains. The largest tree in the world, the General Sherman, is in another grove a hundred miles or so in a different direction. My favorite is the General Grant, the second largest. I can look at the General Grant tree all day long and never get tired of it. It is so unbelievably huge that it takes my breath away. Besides being huge, it is absolutely beautiful.

God's Word is like that for me. I can read it over and over and never get tired of it. It is so awesome it takes my breath away. And it is beautiful beyond description.

From Dunce to Scholar

But it hasn't always been like that. Learning to read my Bible was a struggle for me. Like many of us, I was raised in a church that didn't put any particular emphasis on Bible reading. When I was a new Christian I remember reading Scripture for hours on end, but I missed something back then. Nobody ever encouraged me to read the Bible systematically, and certainly nobody suggested I read it every word of it. Where I came from nobody actually did that. My reading, and that of my Christian friends, was confined to the New Testament and the more readable portions of the Old Testament.

Everything changed the summer after my junior year of college. I wanted to be a missionary, and I'd chosen the perfect mission board. I was in the middle of a summer training course when the most embarrassing thing happened: I flunked a Bible test.

The only test question I remember today had to do with a story I'd never heard of, something about somebody dipping himself in the Jordan River seven times. "Who was he?" I didn't have a clue.

The test results were confidential, so the other missionary candidates never found out what a dunce I was. But *I* knew, and so did the important decision makers in the missionary candidate's office. The powers-that-be told me I needed to attend a year (and possibly more) of Bible school before they would accept my missionary application.

That night the girls in my dorm were chattering about the Bible test. One girl scored 100% and didn't sense a need to be confidential about it. All of them had done well. The thing I remember most about that conversation was this piece of gossip:

"You know, down home in Mississippi," said one of the girls, "there's this guy I used to be interested in, but I broke it off when I learned that he'd never read his Bible. Can you *imagine*? He calls himself a Christian, and he's never even read his Bible all the way through, not even once! Don't y'all think it's *really horrible* to call yourself a Christian if you've never even bothered to read the Bible from cover to cover?"

"Yeah, *really horrible*," agreed all the future missionaries. I felt a bit uncomfortable around my friends that particular evening. These girls were from the Bible belt. I was from California.

When I returned home at the end of the summer I told my pastor about the disastrous Bible test. He commiserated with me for a while, and then I mustered the courage to ask him if he knew a story about a man dipping himself in the Jordan River seven times. I'd tried to find that story but couldn't. There are some things a concordance won't help you with.

"Oh, that was good old Namaan," he said. "He's back there in II Kings somewhere."

My pastor knew the story! And he even knew what book it was in! I was pretty impressed, but then he was a pastor. I was a nobody, so that let me off the hook – for the moment at least. I quickly remembered that Christ had saved me by His blood. So much for the "I was a nobody" excuse.

I quietly admitted to myself that it might be a good idea to read the entire Bible.

I had one more year at Fresno State, so it was back to Anthropology and Linguistics that Fall. There was about a month left before school started, so I did what only college kids on summer vacation can do, and only if they don't have summer jobs. I lounged around my parents' house all day long and I read the entire Bible – from beginning to end for the first time. I did it in one month.

The next summer I returned to my missionary training program and retook the Bible test. I scored so well that the good folks in the missionary candidates' office told me I didn't have to go to Bible school after all.

"We're really impressed," they said. "You must have studied really hard this year. You're suddenly quite a Bible scholar!"

I kept mum and let them think I'd studied hard. Actually, I *had* studied hard my senior year, but I was just doing whatever it took to graduate *summa cum laude*. I also participated in some excellent Bible studies, but that was also my normal routine. Where general Bible knowledge was concerned, the only thing I'd done differently was read the Bible *once* from beginning to end.

Up from Boredom

I never did join that mission board, but a few years later I married N. J. Varughese and joined him on the mission field in India. In the intervening years I'd kept up with Bible reading, but I never could get into a satisfying daily routine. For many years I'd start on January 1 with one of those "Read your Bible in a Year" schedules, but I always get bored and quit by the second week. *Why was Bible reading so boring for me?* I just couldn't understand it. In truth, I loved reading my Bible. I'd pick it up and read it for hours on end, but I only did that when I had a few hours of free time. I wanted desperately to get into a regular routine of daily Bible reading, but why did my love for the Bible evaporate every time I got serious about reading it?

Marrying N.J. Varughese helped me tremendously, because in the early years of our marriage I had more free time than I had had as a single woman. I used it to develop my prayer life and my Bible reading habits. The solution to my Bible reading problem, I discovered, was my *pace*. The once a year routine was boring because it was so ponderously slow! It was like reading the most absorbing novel you can think of, but limiting yourself to three pages a day. For a person with my personality, that was a recipe for boredom for sure!

I used my free time to work out a schedule for reading the Bible in three months, and I actually followed it. I read the Bible through, systematically, for the first time since college. The pace turned out to be too demanding for my time constraints, so I worked out another schedule for reading it in four months, and another for six months.

I still use my old Bible reading schedules. They are really helpful to me. You'll find them on my website.

The True Picture

The first time I read the Bible through from the beginning to end, I read it so quickly that I absorbed it all in one high impact snapshot. And that was an experience I'll never forget. Of course, I cannot share my snapshot with you because the Bible doesn't reproduce well on a photograph.

Here's what I mean: the first time I saw the General Grant tree, I gazed at it for a long time, and I took a picture of it. When I got the negative developed I was heartbroken. It didn't look like the tree at all.

I had inadvertently discovered how difficult the General Grant is to photograph. If you've ever photographed a tall building, you've noticed it comes out looking like a trapezoid. Photos of the General Grant have the same trapezoid effect: a massive trunk and a tiny, wimpy-looking top. In truth, the tree is awesome from top to bottom. The photograph in my mind is far superior to the one I took.

To photograph the General Grant without the trapezoid effect, you would have to get one of those cherry-picker trucks, drive it into the forest, park it a good distance from the tree, lift yourself up to about 150 feet off the ground – and take a picture from that angle. I wonder if anybody has ever done that.

There's only one way to lift yourself off the ground and get a clear "picture" of the Bible in your mind: you'll have to read it from beginning to end. Books about the Bible won't do. Commentaries won't do. Even a difficult Bible survey class won't do. All of these will give you a reasonable, but *fuzzy and distorted*, picture of the Bible. It would be like looking at a photograph of the General Grant instead of looking at the tree itself.

The Panorama of God's Love

The Bible does what no other book can do: it tells the story of mankind from God's perspective. It tells us how God created us, how greatly He loves us, what His plans for us are. It tells about how we sinned against Him and how He reached down from heaven to rescue us from our sinful natures. It tells how evil entered the world and how God will deal with the Evil One in the end.

The Bible starts with the beginning of creation and takes us all the way to the end of life on earth as we know it. Its final chapters give us a glimpse into our eternal future, in heaven with the Lord forever.

The Bible is the only book that contains all of human history, past, present and *future*. Our finest and most learned historians can only give a portrait of the past. Anything they say about the future is conjecture. But the Bible tells us where we have come from, where we are and where we are going.

The Bible is the only book that gives answers to our uniquely human problems. Psychologists try. Philosophers try. Even historians try, yet how many of us actually learn from psychology, philosophy and history? We don't change because human nature forbids us. The Bible teaches us how God can reach down into the depths of our souls and change our very natures.

Read your Bible! When you read it from beginning to end, the *entire panorama* of God's love for mankind will open before you, past, present and future. You'll see life differently. The Bible will teach you the things you need to know to become the person God wants you to be.

Chapter 2

The Artist and the Scientist

Our family took a trip to California this summer. A large part of the trip was planned a year in advance, but just before we set out I made a special request of my husband. Could we please take a little detour up in to the Sierra Nevada Mountains so I could get another look at the Giant Sequoias? It had been a number of years since I had seen them. I was working on this book, and I wanted to refresh my memory.

We made our way into Sequoia National Park and began gaining altitude. When we reached about 6,500 feet, the Giant Sequoias began to appear in the forest near the road. They are unmistakable. You can't miss them because they are so huge and their bark is so very *red*.

We checked out Giant Forest where the General Sherman tree is. We walked around and took a few photographs, and then we drove on to Kings Canyon National Park to see the General Grant, my favorite. The National Park Service has felled some trees so that people can look at it from a distance, which we did. Then we walked up close and picked up a few of its cones from the ground. They were remarkably tiny for such a big tree, only about two inches long. I wanted to walk up next to the tree and touch its bark, but since my last visit the park service had placed fences around all the sequoias. They don't allow us to touch the trees anymore.

In my college days, I would run my hand over the bark. It reminded me of fiberglass because it has the same soft, poufy, airy look. Sequoia bark is two or three feet thick and fireproof, which is why the General Grant has never succumbed to a forest fire in the thousands of years it's been on earth.

That day I walked all the way around General Grant, which I apparently had never done before. I noticed for the first time that the majestic tree had lived through a really massive forest fire perhaps several hundred years ago. General Grant has a huge black scar on its back side, ten or fifteen feet wide and a couple of stories high.

Art Versus Science

In this chapter we are going to examine the difference between Bible reading and Bible study. To do that, consider the difference between art and science.

An artist will stand at a distance, gaze at the General Grant tree and observe its beauty. He'll notice the beautiful reds in its massive trunk. He'll notice the black streaks in the trunk where the forest fires have scorched the bark. He'll follow the trunk's graceful lines upward to notice the lovely contours of the crown. He'll note that the tree is predominantly trunk, and that the proportion of green needles to red bark is surprisingly small. He'll take all this in as his eyes scan the entire tree. He never gets tired of observing the beauty of the tree, because that is what artists love to do.

Bible reading is the artist's approach to the Bible.

A scientist takes a close-up view. He may get fascinated with the structure of the tiny cones. He may want to examine the physical and chemical characteristics of the fireproof bark. Perhaps he'll want to know how sequoia needles differ from those of other conifers. He may pull out a microscope and look at the cell structure of the root hairs. He never gets tired of studying the tree's components because that is what scientists love to do.

Bible study is the scientist's approach to the Bible.

Note that the scientists' studies don't require him to know what the tree looks like. A biology student in some university in Europe may have never seen a giant sequoia. But suppose his professor gives some tiny seeds and says, "These are giant sequoia seeds. Please analyze them." He would analyze the seeds, look at them through a microscope and learn a great deal. He'd get an "A" on his paper, but he wouldn't necessarily know what the tree looked like.

When we study the Bible we take a close look at its various components. On one occasion, we may want to study a book in depth. On another occasion, we may take a topic, say forgiveness, and study that.

We may even feel inclined to take the microscopic approach: there are plenty of Biblical Greek scholars who can't wait to analyze Greek verb usage in the letters of Paul.

Personally, I love Bible study, the more detailed the better. That is the analytical side of my personality. The artist in me loves the panorama of God's Word which I get only through Bible reading.

Nothing "Mere" About It!

I get concerned when I hear comments from those who downplay the importance of Bible reading or make unfair statements about the difference between Bible reading and Bible study. Here are two such comments:

First comment: "Bible study requires rigor, discipline and a pen and paper for taking notes. Without rigor, discipline and notes, you're 'merely reading your Bible.'"

Second comment: "Bible study is superior to Bible reading because if you are 'merely reading your Bible' you are only skimming the surface."

Both of these comments use the phrase, "merely reading your Bible," as though Bible reading were an insignificant activity. Personally, I do not share that view. The Bible is a *long, difficult* book. Reading it from cover to cover is an enormous undertaking. *There is nothing mere about it!*

Rigor, Discipline and Notes

The first comment says that Bible study requires rigor, discipline and a pen and paper. I agree completely. But so does Bible reading.

As you'll see in this book, my approach to systematic Bible reading also involves rigor, discipline and a pen and paper.

So, what is the difference between Bible reading and Bible study? The difference involves *weight.*

Bible reading gives *equal weight* to all portions of Scripture. Bible reading opens our eyes to the entire panorama of God's Word *in the proportion that God gave.* Bible Study singles out segments of Scripture for deeper scrutiny.

Since the Bible is three-fourths Old Testament and one-fourth New Testament, the person who reads it from beginning to end will spend three-fourths of his time reading the Old Testament and one-fourth reading the New Testament. That is the only way we can open our eyes to the entire panorama of God's Word.

If we fail to read the entire Bible we'll be like the biology student who analyzes sequoia seeds without knowing what the tree looks like. We really do need both Bible reading and Bible study if we want to understand God's message to us.

The Cream Always Rises

There was also the second comment that Bible reading is "merely skimming the surface." As I have pointed out, we're not abandoning the deep riches of Bible study simply because we are reading our Bibles. Beyond that, I don't find any problem with skimming the surface. Think about it: what rises to the surface? The cream does!

Whether we study the Bible's various components in depth, or whether we "merely read it," the most we will ever do is skim off the cream that God wants to give us. No matter how deeply we delve into our Bibles, we'll come away with the understanding that we were merely skimming the surface.

Remember: All Knowledge is Too Deep to Comprehend

Knowledge, by its very nature, is too deep for us mortals to comprehend. This is true of Bible knowledge as well as any other kind of knowledge under the sun.

When one of my Linguistics buddies finished her PhD, she told me about a fellow student who came down with a severe case of self-doubt. He was aware that in his PhD program he had merely skimmed the surface of what there was to learn about Linguistics. He had been offered a job as a professor, but he was on the verge of turning it down because he didn't think he knew enough about Linguistics! My friend patted him on the back and told him to take the job because he had just been awarded a PhD from a prestigious university. He knew quite a bit about Linguistics after all.

God structured the universe in such a way that whether you study Linguistics, Chemistry, Medicine, Astronomy, Mathematics or History you never come to the place where you feel like you know much beyond surface knowledge.

Think about it: if Mathematics is deep, how much deeper is the very Word of God? A dedicated Bible scholar, who has spent an entire lifetime studying the depths of God's Word, knows that he has only skimmed the surface. That's how deep the riches of God's Word really are.

So, don't worry about merely skimming the surface. We are unapologetically doing exactly that. Our purpose here is to learn everything we possibly can from the surface view of the Bible.

You'll find as I have that every time you read your Bible you'll skim something different off the top. Cream will rise each time. But it will be new cream each time. It will be special cream that God has put there just for you. It will be just exactly the right cream that you need on any given day for your spiritual journey with Him.

Read your Bible!

Chapter 3

Personality, Values and Time

I was taking my regular morning walk a while back when something exciting happened. My walking time is when the Lord and I do business. I ask Him what he wants me to do that day, He gives me instructions and I do my best to go home and follow them. On that particular day I had extra special, exciting instructions. I was to write the book you now see on Bible reading. So, I went home and started writing.

A few days later I phoned a close friend and told her about my project. I explained to her that I had Bible reading schedules for reading the Bible in 3 months, 4 months, 6 months, etc. She didn't like my idea very much. She told me she *wouldn't dream* of reading her Bible in less than two or three years.

My husband is the same way. He finds it extremely satisfying to read one or two chapters a day and stick with it for however long it takes to read the Bible through. It can easily take him three years. If that were me (with my personality), I'd be fighting frustration by the end of the first week. Genesis is so exciting that I really want to push on to see how it ends. Of course I already know how it ends, but I can't wait to read it again and again.

These are personality issues. When you get down to the nitty-gritty of systematic Bible reading, you'll quickly learn how personal the activity is.

There are three things you'll need to consider when you set up your personal Bible reading program. The first is your personality. The other two are your values and your time constraints. You'll want to develop a program that works for your unique set of circumstances in all three areas.

My burden is to help people everywhere get into the habit of reading the Bible systematically, every word, over and over for the rest of their lives, no matter what their unique circumstances may be. So I've tried to include a little something for everybody. When you look at the strategies and schedules available, evaluate them and work out a program that suits your unique personality, values and time issues.

Here are some points that apply to everyone.

What is Systematic Bible Reading?

Systematic Bible reading is what I advocate, and the key word of course is *systematic*. It is not just helter-skelter, here and there reading. It has structure and two important goals.

The *first* goal is to read every word. To do this, it's important to keep track of where you are. I don't always read the Bible straight through. Sometimes I skip around a bit, so I use check boxes to remind me of what I have and haven't read.

The *second* goal is to read in the proportion that God gave. In my Bible reading program I don't read any book or chapter twice until I have read the entire Bible through. I do, however, study the Bible as well as read it, so I may be studying a book – reading that book over and over – while I concurrently read the Bible. But I consider Bible study a separate activity from Bible Reading.

So, these are the two components of systematic Bible reading:

1. Read every word
2. Read in the proportion that God gave.

Fast or Slow?

Whether you read your Bible quickly or slowly is a matter of values. My husband values the meditative aspect of Bible reading. I value the impact of the seeing the entire Bible unfold before my eyes.

My husband's approach gives short shrift to the unfolding drama of the entire counsel of God. My approach gives less time for meditating over important passages. These are values issues.

Whether you prefer the fast approach or the slow approach, I really think everyone should read the Bible through quickly at least once in their lives (by quickly, I mean in six months or less). The main reason is the dramatic effect of seeing God's Word altogether in one snapshot. I've already gone over this, so here are some other reasons why rapid reading is effective.

Rapid reading keeps you in constant touch with the Word of God. I remember talking with a friend about the story of Moses being put in a basket when he was a baby. She was amazed at the detail in my memory of that story. Actually, I'm not as smart as she may have thought. The truth is I'd just read that story that morning. If it had been two years since I'd read Exodus, I guarantee my memory would have been a great deal more fuzzy.

Rapid reading is an effective platform for further Bible study. Once I was interested in studying all the prayers of the Bible. It was really frustrating trying to locate them all using a concordance or other Bible help. I found it easier to just note them down as I came to them in my reading.

For each pass through the Bible, you might try to jot down all the instances of something. Old Testament references to the blood of Jesus might be an interesting topic. References to angels could be another. You'll find this technique to be a marvelous springboard for further study, but it won't work if it takes you three years to read your Bible.

Rapid reading doesn't have to preclude meditation. Let's be honest here: if you have the time to read your Bible in, say, six months, then you also have time to meditate on it. If you can find the time to read seven chapters in a day, then you can also find 15 minutes to meditate on one of those chapters. It depends on your values.

Don't ever neglect meditative reading. When you read the Bible, always choose a passage to meditate on before the Lord.

The Time Factor

Your personal time factor plays a large role in your Bible reading strategy. I have a friend who cares for a husband and seven children and works full time. She once told me quite honestly that she doesn't have time for much of a devotional life. She's exactly right about that. But the Lord knows her heart and He strengthens her every day in marvelous ways. In spite of her time constraints, she walks very closely with the Lord every moment of her day.

I don't walk in her shoes, so I can find time to read my Bible.

Most people have more time than they think they have. If you watch television for an hour a day or more, then you have time to read your Bible for an hour a day or more. Again it's a matter of values.

Carry your Bible with you. This is easy, because we can download it on our cell phones. Have your phone charged and ready to go when you're at the beauty parlor, the doctor's office or anywhere else. Read your Bible during your lunch hour. Always carry it with you.

Spread your reading throughout the day. My day doesn't always allow for a long stretch of time for reading and yours may not either. Read a little bit in the morning when you get up. During the day if you need a break from whatever you're doing, read another couple of chapters. Be alert to the various lulls that occur during your day and have your Bible handy. By evening, you'll be done, or perhaps another few minutes will be enough to finish the day's reading goal before you retire.

Spreading your reading out throughout the day has a terrific advantage in that you are never far from the Word. You'll find yourself thinking about it as you go about your day far more than if you read it in one session in the morning.

It doesn't take as much time as you think. This was the thing that amazed me the most when I started reading my Bible again after a pause of a few years. I chose a four month schedule, and I was prepared for a real struggle finding the time. I discovered it wasn't the time that was the problem, it was the inclination. In the beginning I was in a "this is going to be tough" mood. Those are the kinds of moods that cause me to give up before I get started. But once I got myself going I discovered that it took much less time that I originally thought it would.

Time flies when you're having a good time. After a couple of weeks I really started enjoying reading my Bible. Time wasn't a factor at all when I found myself really wanting to read my Bible. Again, this goes back to values.

Every Day?

No, I really don't think you need to make systematic Bible reading a rigid part of every single day of your life. Some days you'll be sick. Some days will get away from you because of travel. Some days you'll have an emergency you have never dreamed of. Some days, if you're like me, you'll be downright lazy or rebellious (just being honest here).

Repent of laziness and rebellion, but otherwise don't beat yourself up if you slide once in a while. In fact, all of my Bible reading schedules have built-in catch-up days. I put these in many years ago because I discovered I needed them. I was always falling behind for one reason or another and the catch-up days really helped.

I don't really think that systematic reading needs to be a relentlessly ongoing ritual. If you like variety, you might want to choose a six-month plan for the first half of the year. For the second half of the year, take a break from rigorous Bible reading so you can get to that study of Romans you've wanted to do. Don't allow yourself to get burned out reading your Bible.

So it all depends on your unique set of circumstances. But I can say this about myself: I've committed myself to systematic Bible reading over and over again for the rest of my life.

To Sum Up

Are you ready to start reading? If so, work out a Bible reading strategy that suits your unique personality, values and time constraints. Ask yourself these two questions:

- How much time can I realistically devote to Bible reading?
- Am I a fast reader or a slow reader?

When you have answered these questions, you'll be able develop a reading program that is perfect for you. If you are a fast reader and you have an hour a day, you could go for a three-month schedule. If you only have 15 minutes per day, consider a year-long schedule.

If you are super slow like my husband and friend, you won't even need a schedule. Just read (and meditate) for however long you wish. Put down your Bible for the day and pick up where you left off the next day. Take all the time you want to read your Bible through.

Chapter 4

The Bible Reader's Creed

Sometimes people ask me how I stay motivated to read my Bible over and over. To be honest, I haven't always been motivated. After my first read-through in college, there was a pause of a number of years before I read it the second time.

When I started reading it again, I realized what I had been missing by concentrating on Bible study only. That is when I began to understand the difference between Bible reading and Bible study. I wrote the Bible Reader's Creed for myself, and I have been following it as faithfully as I can ever since.

With God's help, I will read my Bible,
every word, in the proportion that God gave,
over and over again, for the rest of my life.

Here are the elements of the creed, spelled out:

With God's Help

I discovered quickly that if I try to read the Bible simply for the sake of reading, or simply to finish my reading goal for the day, I would quickly get burned out. Always depend on the Lord you help you through.

I Will Read My Bible

I had to discipline myself to *reading* the Bible, not getting side-tracked by Bible study. This was hard in the beginning because I was always coming across passages that I wanted to learn more about. These days, I simply make a note of what I'd like to take a deeper look at, and I keep reading. The "deeper look" comes under the subject of Bible study which is a separate activity from Bible reading.

Every Word

God gave us the entire Bible, every word inspired. God wants us to read His Word, all of it.

All Scripture is given by inspiration of God, and is profitable for doctrine, for reproof, for correction, for instruction in righteousness.   *(II Tim 3:16)*

I've been tempted to skip over boring passages, and in the past I would do exactly that. Through the years, I've become more disciplined in this area. I make it a point to read every word of those boring genealogies, and every word of the Jewish legal code. It's all there for a purpose.

Honestly, I've come to a point where I'm not nearly as bored as I used to be. Everything in the Bible fascinates me now, and I believe that is part of God's enabling.

In the Proportion that God Gave

The Bible is three-fourths Old Testament and one-fourth New Testament. When we read the entire Bible from beginning to end, we spend three-fourths of our time reading the Old Testament and one-fourth of our time reading the New Testament.

Over and Over Again

Back in college, when I read the Bible through for the first time, I mentally put a giant tick mark next to the "I have read the entire Bible" entry on my list of accomplishments, and I didn't read it again for a while.

These days I read the Word over and over again. When I finish Revelation, I begin again with Genesis. I'm a fast reader, but my husband, the slow reader, does the same thing. It may take him two or three years to get through the entire Bible, but then he starts over again with Genesis.

For the Rest of My Life

I plan on making Bible reading a feature of my walk with God for the rest of my life. It's like bathing in a refreshing pond, and I just love the Word!

Chapter 5

And Then, There's the Why

So, let's get this question off our minds: Why should we read the Bible?

I suppose the easiest answer is because God wants us to. He gave us the Bible after all, and why would He do that unless He wants us to read it?

But for further reasons, just check the internet, and you'll find endless lists of reasons we should read the Bible. Things like,

- to know God
- to live a better life
- to keep ourselves from sin, etc, etc, etc.

The problem is that almost anybody could sit down and mindlessly rattle off a dozen reasons, and none of them would be wrong. There is no wrong reason to read the Bible.

Boiler plate answers tend to bore me, so I decided to reframe the question and ask it again at a more personal level. Why DO people read the Bible? Why does John read it, or George, or Pete or Kristen?

I asked John why he read the Bible, and here's what he told me. "I was sitting in front of the TV watching football one Sunday afternoon, and a tremendous sense of conviction came over me. I turned off the television and picked up my Bible. Since then I've read it more than 50 times."

George lost his wife. In tremendous grief he looked to the Lord, then picked up his Bible and started reading. He's been reading his Bible ever since.

Pete was facing financial problems, health problems, relationship problems, and nearly every kind of problem known to man. He was even into pornography big time. Pete had been a Christian his entire adult life, but he couldn't understand why he wasn't living victoriously in the Lord. In desperation, Pete began seeking the Lord like never before – and in the process he started reading his Bible seriously for the first time. Gradually, as he read, God's truths spoke to him and led him through the storm. Today, Pete has overcome his problems, he lives a victorious life in Christ, and he still reads his Bible.

Kristen has been reading her Bible ever since she could read. The house rules were: get up, get dressed, brush your teeth, make your bed, read your Bible, eat breakfast, go to school. After school the rules were: do your homework, read your Bible, go out and play. At bedtime, the family always read the Bible together, and then the kids brushed their teeth and went to bed. Kristen still reads her Bible faithfully and teaches her children to read as well.

Unless you had parents like Kristen's parents, there is a very good chance that a *crisis* is what got you going. In my case, I was shamed into reading my Bible because I'd flunked a Bible test. Everybody's reason for starting a reading program is a bit different, but once the personal journey begins, people seldom quit.

When you reach the point where you're committed to reading the Bible, *then* you can go to the internet and read all the reasons you're supposed to. You may relate to some of them better than others, but your personal reasons will be unique to you.

In the end, Bible reading involves a commitment to change. John gave up football, George adjusted to life without his sweetheart, Pete made a concerted effort to turn his life around.

And Kristen? She was well trained as a child, but at some point, she moved out of her parent's home, got married and started a family. She made a conscious *adult* decision to saturate herself in God's Word each day – and she is teaching her children the same way.

You can bring about a change in your daily routine by picking up your Bible and reading it.

Then, stand back and watch how profoundly the Bible changes *you!*

Part II

Bible Basics

Chapter 6

For the Absolute Beginner: Books, Chapters and Verses

If you are totally unfamiliar with the Bible, I suggest you turn to the Table of Contents at the beginning. You'll notice straightaway that there are two major sections, the Old Testament and the New Testament. These are sometimes referred to as the Old Covenant and the New Covenant. Both the Old and New Testaments cover historical periods that took place in specific geographic locations.

The Old Testament is the story of the Jewish people, God's chosen people, from creation up until the sixth century BC. The setting is in the Middle East, mostly Israel. Some events occur in what is now modern-day Egypt, Iraq and Syria. The Old Testament was written in the Hebrew language.

The New Testament begins with the birth of Jesus Christ. Events in the New Testament are placed in the Middle East and Southern Europe, and cover only about 100 years of history, the life span of Jesus and His disciples. The last of His twelve disciples to die was John who died in 100 AD. The New Testament was written in the Greek language.

One of the major differences between Christianity and Judaism is that Jews only recognize the Old Testament as Scripture. Christians believe that Jesus is the Messiah and therefore recognize both the Old and New Testaments.

Lots of Books with Strange Names

Look at the table of contents again and you'll find a list of strange names, Genesis, Exodus, Leviticus, etc. These are called *books,* and Genesis is the first book in the Bible. There are 39 books in the Old Testament, and 27 books in the New Testament, or 66 in all. These books were written by about 40 different authors over a period of some 1540 years. All sixty-six books make up the Bible.

The first book to be written is thought to be Job. We don't know when it was written or who the author was. The last book written was Revelation, which is also the last book of the Bible. It was written by John, one of Jesus' disciples, in about 95 AD.

Each book of the Bible has its own flavor and character, central theme and purpose. But taken as a whole, all sixty-six books come together as one cohesive, awe-inspiring story.

Chapters and Verses

The Bible is a very long book, and it's easy to get lost. To keep track of where things can be found, a man named Stephen Langton set about to divide each book into *chapters*. He started this project in the year 1227 in England and spent many years on it before he finished. We continue to use his chapter divisions today.

Somewhat later, another Bible scholar divded Langton's chapters into *verses*. All Bibles today are divded into chapters and verses.

Here's how it works. Open your Bible to the first book, Genesis (find the page number in the table of contents). You'll see the number *1* in big, bold print, followed by the words, "In the beginning God created the heavens and the earth." Then you will see the number *2* written in a small superscript type. This will be followed by the words, "The earth was without form, and void..."

It will look something like this:

1 In the beginning God created the heavens and the earth. ² The earth was without form, and void ...

You may have a different translation, but the system will be the same. The bold numbers are called *chapter numbers* and the smaller numbers are *verse numbers*.

Now scan down though the page. After verse 31 you will come to the number **2** in large, bold print. This is the beginning of Genesis, chapter 2. Scan down through chapter 2, and after verse 25 you will come to chapter 3. Chapter 1 has 31 verses and chapter 2 has twenty-five verses. How many verses does chapter 3 have?

Not all chapters have the same number of verses. Some chapters are short and others are long. Scholars set up the system hundreds of years ago. It works pretty well, even today.

Chapters and verses are referred to using the following format: book name (usually abbreviated) followed by the chapter number, then a colon, then the verse number. Here are some examples:

> Gen 1:1   (Genesis chapter 1, verse 1)
> Prov 3:5-6   (Proverbs chapter 3, verses 5 through 6)
> Phil 4:4   (Philippians chapter 4, verse 4)

To get a feel for how this works, look these Bible verses up. If you have trouble finding a book, use the table of contents. Then find the chapter and verse and read what it says. For good measure check out the most famous verse in the Bible, John 3:16.

By the way, these are good verses to commit to memory.

You'll Catch on in No Time

Finding your way around the Bible can be a challenge for first time readers. Don't be afraid to ask a friend for help! In time (actually, not much time), the Bible will be easy to navigate, and you won't need to use the table of contents. All the books, chapters and verses will become your close friends before you know it.

Chapter 7

The Bible's Central Message

The Bible opens with the story of creation. God created the heavens, the earth, the sun, moon, stars, the oceans, the dry land, the plants and all the animals. Last, he created Adam and Eve, the first humans.

Adam and Eve were in a perfect relationship with God. This perfect relationship was (and still is!) God's plan for mankind. Things went wrong when Adam and Eve sinned. You'll read about what happened in Genesis, chapter 3.

God cannot tolerate sin in His presence, so when Adam and Eve sinned, their perfect relationship with God was severed.

The rest of the Bible has one central theme, God's desire to restore fellowship with mankind.

The Bible's Central Message

The Bible is the story of God's unrelenting effort to restore a perfect relationship between Himself and mankind

---

Yes, it's true. God wants us to be with Him in a perfect relationship. Did you ever wish you had a perfect relationship with your earthly father? Maybe you had a great father. Perhaps you had an abusive father, a drunken father, an absent father, or no father at all. It doesn't matter. Every father on earth has had his share of shortcomings, and we've all had to adapt accordingly.

The good news is that you have a Father in heaven who has no faults. He loves you and wants a perfect relationship with you. A day never goes by when He is not yearning for you, wanting to be with you.

The Bible tells the story of how God made a provision for complete fellowship with Him. Many people call it "God's plan of salvation."

God laid out His plan of salvation in a step-by-step historical process which the Bible traces eloquently. I'll give a brief overview by explaining three of the covenants God made with mankind as a part of this restoration process (there are more than three covenants in the Bible, but I'll briefly explain three of them here.)

A covenant is a binding legal contract between two parties. In the covenants I'm sharing here, God (who initiated these covenants) is the one party. The other party is the person or group of people that He made the covenant with. Each party has terms that they are obligated to. The covenant becomes official when it is "sealed" by an animal sacrifice in which blood is shed.

It's important to understand that *all covenants* between God and man require a blood sacrifice in order for the contract to become legally binding.

God's Covenant with Abraham

God made a covenant with a man named Abraham about 4,000 years ago. The terms were simple and easy to understand.

- From God's side, He would make Abraham's descendants a great nation, His chosen people.

- From Abraham's side, he and his descendants' throughout all time would circumcise their male children.

The Abrahamic covenant was sealed when Abraham sacrificed a heifer, a female goat, a ram, a turtledove and a young pigeon before the Lord. Through this covenant, God established Abraham's descendants as His chosen people through whom he would work out His magnificent plan of salvation.

Abraham's descendants still exist today. They are known as Jews. Every Jew who has ever lived is a direct descendant of Abraham. Even today in the 21st century, Jews exist as a separate, unique people, and they still circumcise their male children.

God's Covenant with Moses

About 400 years after that, Abraham's descendants had grown to about 3 million people and God made another covenant with them. This time He gave them the law (a set of rules and regulations) and instructed them to follow it.

This covenant is referred to as the Mosaic Covenant (named after a man named Moses). Since it is the major covenant of the Old Testament, it is often simply referred to as the Old Covenant. It also was sealed through blood sacrifices of animals.

Again, the terms were easy to understand:

- From God's side He would bring the Jews into the Promised Land and continue to make them his chosen people.

- From the children of Israel's side, they were to obey the law.

There was one problem with the Old Covenant: the children of Israel couldn't live up to its terms. Nobody could obey the law flawlessly. The people broke the covenant with God.

In response, God, in His unrelenting efforts to restore mankind to Himself, devised a new way to make restoration possible.

Jeremiah and the New Covenant

Another thousand years went by. By this time there were prophets in Israel who foretold the future. They began talking about a Messiah who would come and redeem Israel. One of these prophets was a man named Jeremiah who declared that a New Covenant was coming.

*Behold, the days are coming, says the Lord, when I will make a **new covenant** with the house of Israel and with the house of Judah ...   (Jer 31:31)*

When was this prophecy fulfilled? The Old Testament ends rather poignantly with the promise of the Messiah and the New Covenant. Today the Jews are still waiting for their Messiah.

The New Covenant Fulfilled in Jesus Christ

We Christians believe that this prophecy was fulfilled when Jesus came. Jesus is the Messiah. He is the One who established the New Covenant with His blood.

On the night before the crucifixion, Jesus was in a room with His disciples celebrating the annual Jewish Passover feast. He lifted up the Passover Cup and said,

> *This cup is the new covenant in My blood, which is shed for*
> *you.*   *(Luke 22:20)*

This simple statement must have stirred deep emotions in His Jewish disciples. They knew very well that their people had been waiting for the New Covenant for about six hundred years (since Jeremiah's prophecy).

Instead of being sealed by the blood of an *animal* sacrifice, the New Covenant was sealed by the blood of Jesus. His death on the cross was the blood sacrifice that all covenants require.

Again, the terms were easy to understand:

- From God's side He would sacrifice His only son, Jesus, to restore us to fellowship with Him.

- From our side, all we have to do is repent from our sins and believe in Jesus.

The terms couldn't be easier! All we have to do is believe in Jesus. God does the rest.

The Old Covenant was based on man's ability to follow the law, and no one was able to do that. The New Covenant is based only on God's lovingkindness and favor which we do not deserve.

The Old Covenant was given to the Jews. The New Covenant is offered freely to every man, woman and child in every corner of the earth, to everyone who believes in the Lord Jesus.

Our Magnificent Future

Through Christ, God's plan of salvation is complete except for one detail: we still live on this earth where there is a great deal of evil all around us. When we are finished with our lives on earth, we will receive our eternal reward and dwell in the house of the Lord forever.

The Bible concludes with a magnificent vision of heaven. Heaven is the place where we will spend all of eternity with Him. It is the place where there is no evil, where there is no sin, where there are no tears, where the streets are made of pure gold, and where there is no sun or moon because the glory of the Lord provides light.

Heaven is the place where we will spend eternity in a perfect relationship with God – the very relationship He has desired with mankind since Adam and Eve sinned against Him.

Chapter 8

Different Kinds of Books

Is one book of the Bible just like another? No, definitely not.

Scholars have divided Bible books into five classifications according to their content. These classifications are *history, poetry, prophecy, gospels* and *epistles*, which I will explain below. As you read your Bible, the differences between these classifications of books will become obvious to you.

Old Testament Classifications

In the Old Testament there are three classifications of books: *history* books, *poetry* books and *prophecy* books.

History Books. The first section of books in the Bible are classified as the *historical* books of the Bible and are sometimes called the *narrative* books of the Bible. These books were written in prose, as opposed to poetry. Generally speaking, prose is easy to read.

The historical books, from Genesis to Esther, cover nearly half of the Bible.

Yes, these books are all about history, specifically the history of the Jewish people. Why the Jews? Because they are God's chosen people. You'll read about how God called a man named Abraham to be the father of the Jews, and about how salvation is from the Jews.

The first five books of the Bible (Genesis, Exodus, Leviticus, Numbers and Deuteronomy) have a sub-classification called the *Pentateuch*, which means "five books." These books are historical in nature, but they also contain the Jewish legal code interspersed with the historical narrative. These five books are sometimes called the *Books of Moses* because they were written by Moses. Jews refer to these five books as the *Torah.*

Poetry books. The Old Testament also has five books of poetry (Psalms, Proverbs, Ecclesiastes, Song of Solomon and Lamentations). These books were originally cast in poetry and are mainly devotional and instructional in nature. They were written during the period of Jewish history when the Jews were ruled by kings. In fact, King David himself wrote many of the poems that are recorded in the book of Psalms.

Prophecy books. There are 16 books of prophecy in the Old Testament. Some of these were written during the era of kings and others were written during and shortly after the Babylonian captivity. Prophecy books are further sub-divided into *Major Prophets* (Isaiah, Jeremiah, Ezekiel and Daniel) and *Minor Prophets* (the remaining 12 prophecy books, Hosea through Malachi)

All the books of the Old Testament can be broadly classified into history, poetry or prophecy books. The only book that defies strict classification is the book of Job. It is written in poetry but is very different from the other poetry books and is sometimes classified with the history books.

New Testament Classifications

The remaining two classifications, *gospels* and *epistles,* are only found in the New Testament.

Gospels. The word *gospel* means "good news." The first four books of the New Testament (Matthew, Mark, Luke, and John) are called *gospels* because they tell the good news of Jesus Christ. These books are short, biographical sketches that trace the life of Christ from His birth to His death and resurrection.

When Jesus lived on the earth, He healed the sick, raised the dead, gave sermons, told stories (which are called *parables* in the Bible), but He never wrote anything. Everything about what He did was communicated by word of mouth in the beginning, but as time went by, there was a tremendous need to document the life and ministry of Jesus.

The first gospel writer was Mark who wrote about 30 years after Jesus' resurrection. Matthew and Luke followed soon after and drew extensively from Mark. These three gospels are called the synoptic gospels because they follow similar outlines and have many features in common. The fourth gospel, written by John, was written sometime later and differs in content from the first three. All four gospels were written in the first century AD.

The gospels are not continuations of one another. That is, Mark doesn't start where Matthew leaves off. Each of them is a complete stand-alone account of the life of Jesus. They all explain what He did when he walked on the earth and they all tell the about His death and resurrection. Two of them also include the story of His birth.

Epistles. The New Testament also contains 21 *epistles*, which is a fancy word for *letters*. These books are a series of letters from prominent Christian leaders to churches and individuals. They were all written in the 1st century.

The New Testament also contains one history book (Acts) and one prophecy book (Revelation). There are no poetry books in the New Testament.

To sum up, there are five classifications of books in the Bible: *history, poetry, prophecy, gospels* and *epistles*. There is also the *Pentateuch*, the first five books of the Old Testament, which is a subset of the history books.

Chapter 9

A Word on Translations

As you may know, the Old Testament was originally written in ancient Hebrew, and the New Testament was written in Koine Greek (a dialect that is similar to Classical Greek). Nobody speaks these languages today, so we rely on translations. You'll need to choose a good one for your Bible reading program.

We are blessed because our native language is English, and we have many versions of the Bible to choose from.

King James, the All-Time Favorite

The most cherished translation into English was published in 1611. King James I of England commissioned a committee of scholars to write a translation that would be authorized to be read in the churches of England. They came up with what is known today as the *King James Version,* abbreviated KJV.

This translation was written 400 years ago, during the same time that Shakespeare (who died in 1616) was writing. By the time the 20th century rolled around, English had changed so much that Shakespeare was getting difficult for people to read – and so was the Bible.

By the middle of the 20th century, fresh translations began to appear. Although many Christians are satisfied with modern translations, there are some staunch KJV lovers who refuse to read anything else. In fact, KJV is still the most commonly owned and used translation in the United States.

For myself, I'm very fond of the King James Version. I've read it so often that the "thees" and "thous" don't bother me. But to be perfectly honest, King James is a difficult read, even for me.

If you are from a denomination that insists on King James, you can learn to read it. All you have to do is exercise determination. But the modern translations are, without doubt, far more readable.

Translations and Paraphrases

English Bible editions fall into two broad categories: *translations* and *paraphrases*.

Translations are designed for accuracy. That is, the translators try their best to render an exact translation of the original text. The problem is that "exactness" is not possible since certain words, phrases and grammatical forms don't have exact equivalents in English.

The trick is to come up with a translation that is accurate on the one hand, and which makes grammatical and lexical sense to English readers on the other. It's not easy. Today we have some excellent modern translations into English. All of them have strengths and weakness, but all of them strive to be as accurate as possible and are quite reliable.

Paraphrases became popular in the latter part of the 20th century when people decided to sacrifice accuracy for *readability*. The theory was that the Bible was "too hard to read," so the idea of the Bible paraphrase was born.

The author of a paraphrase attempts to figure out the *meaning* of a portion of Scripture and asks himself, "How would I say this in plain, simple English?" What he comes up with is not a translation of the Bible, but his own *interpretation,* written in his own version of plain, simple English.

Various paraphrases were published in the 20th century, but the phenomenon really took off in 1971 when Kenneth Taylor published *The Living Bible*. It was an instant best seller.

I am not a big fan of paraphrases for two reasons:

First, in my opinion, the difficulty in understanding the Bible isn't just the fault of the translation. The problem lies in the difficult *content* of the Bible. Let's be honest here. There are concepts in the Bible that challenge our comprehension – regardless of the translation.

Here's the truth about difficult content: God didn't explain everything to us. Regarding certain concepts, He only told us *everything He wants us to know at this time.* The rest we will learn in due time.

If you are reading an accurate translation of a difficult passage of Scripture, you are reading *everything God said* in that passage. If you put on your scholar's hat and study the original Greek or Hebrew, the most you could do is evaluate the translation. But you would still only know *everything God said* in that passage.

Folks, take note: it is impossible to accurately expand on *everything God said!*

In short, God doesn't always spell out the deeper meaning in difficult passages. But paraphrase advocates still can't resist the urge to make the Bible "easy to read." They do this by adding explanatory words and phrases here and there that are not found in the original text.

The *second* reason I'm not fond of paraphrases is that they tend to use contemporary idioms and slang. The problem is that idioms and slang change with every generation. By contrast, God's Word was set down in Greek and Hebrew over 2,000 years ago, and the original text has never changed.

An accurate translation cares nothing about American slang. The goal is to accurately translate *everything God said* in any given passage without adding any unnecessary words or interpretations.

I won't belabor the point further except to quote I Peter 2:2:

as newborn babes, desire the pure milk of the word, that you may grow...   *(I Peter 2:2)*

The key word here is "pure." I urge you to use an authoritative, accurate, *pure* translation and not a paraphrase.

So, What's the Final Verdict?

Among the most popular reliable translations today are New International Version, New King James Version, English Standard Version, New American Standard Version and the Christian Standard Bible. I have read all of these in their entirety, and my favorite might be the English Standard Version.

I say *might be* because I really can't decide, and I continue to love my trusty King James Version. All of them are suitable for Bible reading.

Chapter 10

Where and How to Begin

Now we come to where the rubber meets the road. You need to actually read your Bible! Before you start, commit yourself to the Bible Reader's Creed:

With God's help, I will read my Bible,
every word, in the proportion that God gave,
over and over again for the rest of my life.

Next, discern your personality, values and time. What kind of personality do you have? What are your time constraints? You can review Chapter 3 as you give this some thought.

Chose a schedule that fits your personality, values and time constraints. I have several schedules on my website, and there are hundreds available online. When you find one, resolve to stick with it until you are finished with that read-through.

Chose a time of day and make it a regular feature of your daily routine. By the way, you do have a daily routine, don't you? If you don't, it might be something to work on.

In my current routine I have several things that I try to accomplish every morning, and one of them is to read my Bible for 30 minutes. I chose 30 minutes because it works for me. That's the only reason.

When 30 minutes is up, I move on to another activity. Sometimes I've finished my reading goal for the day and sometimes I haven't. In the evening I try to have a time of devotions before I go to bed, and that's when I finish my Bible reading goal if necessary.

Feel free to use any time of day that works for you, but try to be consistent.

Next, choose a good translation. I have some recommendations in my chapter on Bible translations. Please don't use a paraphrase as your primary reading Bible.

Lastly, I recommend that you begin at the beginning and read straight through. For a number of years, I would split things up into four segments. Every day I would read something from each of the following categories: History, Poetry, Prophesy and New Testament. It was a system that I used for many years, and there's nothing wrong with it if it suits your personality.

In more recent years I've been reading straight through from Genesis to Revelation, and then starting over. For me personally, I have found this to be the most satisfying approach.

Some Bible teachers recommend starting with the New Testament. They point out that people who begin with Genesis seldom finish the Bible. His point is well taken because most people who start with Genesis wash out somewhere in Exodus or Leviticus.

But to be honest, I don't see much of a difference between starting with Genesis or with the New Testament. My hunch is that even people who start with the New Testament wash out somewhere in Exodus or Leviticus. And when do these people get around to reading Nahum?

Yes, the Bible has books that are difficult to read – no matter where you begin reading. But that is the very reason I've written this book. I want to help you get through the difficult portions so that you can read God's entire Word with confidence.

You'll do well. Pick a translation, a schedule, and start today!

Part III

Tips on How to Read the Bible

Chapter 11

How to Get the Most Out of Reading Your Bible

In the following chapters we will give a few tips on reading the various forms of Scripture. As you'll see, reading a poetry book is not at all like reading a book of prophecy. Reading Job is not at all like reading Revelation.

But first, here are a few tips that apply to all forms of Scripture. They will help you read the entire Bible effectively.

Read Systematically

As I have explained earlier, my concept of Systematic Bible Reading has two factors:

1. Read every word
2. Read in the proportion that God gave

When we read the Bible, we don't skip the parts that are boring or difficult to understand. We read the entire Bible, every word.

Also, we give equal weight to all passages. On any given read-through, we read all books once before reading any book a second time. This practice assures that we honor the proportion that God gave us.

That said, it is important that we not neglect Bible study which can be done simultaneously.

Always be Thinking of Jesus

As we have seen in Chapter 7, the Bible is the story of God's unrelenting effort to restore a perfect relationship between Himself and mankind. He sent Jesus Christ to restore that relationship by dying for us on the cross.

Always be thinking of Jesus when you read your Bible. The entire Old Testament leads to the coming of the Messiah, the birth, death and resurrection of our Lord, Jesus Christ. The first reference to Him is in Genesis 3:15 when God says to the serpent,

> *And I will put enmity*
> *Between you and the woman,*
> *And between your seed and her Seed;*
> *He shall bruise your head,*
> *And you shall bruise His heel. (Genesis 3:15)*

Who is the seed of the woman? Jesus is. You'll find hundreds of references to Jesus when you read the Old Testament. Many of them will be obscure, but the Lord will open your eyes to them as you read your Bible.

And of course, the New Testament is all about Jesus. No obscurity here! Always be thinking of Him. Always be drawing closer to Him, loving Him more and more each day.

Read Respectfully

I remember a certain Bible reading moment when I was in college. I read a passage (I no longer remember which passage), and I said to myself, "I don't agree with that," and I gave myself a list of reasons which made sense at the time.

Back then, I subjected all of my reading to some serious critical thinking. Whether it was literature, history or psychology, I filtered everything through certain criteria in my mind before accepting any idea or principle set forth in whatever I was reading.

On that particular day, it occurred to me that I wasn't reading Shakespeare or Freud. I was reading the Word of God. The critical thinking filters I'd set up simply didn't apply to the Bible. When we read the Bible, we look to God as our teacher. Our job is to learn, not to argue.

Read Confidently

When I was a child, I remember somebody saying, "God said it, I believe it, that settles it!" Today I regard it as a cute jingle, but I don't appreciate the lack of reasoning behind it. Some people can be quite lazy when it comes to any sort of deep thinking.

The fact is that all of us have struggled with portions of scripture. Did God really create the earth in seven days? Did Jesus really die on the cross? Is homosexuality really a sin? I once knew a man who didn't believe in hell. A loving God wouldn't send anybody there, he said. Believe or not, he was a pastor.

Don't be afraid to wrestle with issues that stir up deep emotions in your soul. Think deeply about what your core beliefs are. Let the Bible challenge you.

At the same time, read with confidence. Know with certainty that God is speaking truth through His Word. Jesus said,

> *If you abide in My word, you are My disciples indeed. And you shall know the truth, and the truth shall make you free.*
> *(John 8:31-32)*

When you genuinely understand that God is teaching you truth, you'll find it so much easier to believe the Bible, all of it, with confidence.

Read Meditatively

Meditative reading is an art we will master as we go along. We must be attentive and humble as we read. We must listen as the Holy Spirit speaks to us. We must brood over we what He says.

In short, we pray as we read, always asking Him to teach us what we need to know.

Bible teachers often talk about the importance of "applying" the Scriptures to our daily lives. I never could get a grasp on what that meant. The concept wasn't personal enough for me, something like applying butter to a piece of toast.

These days I just ask myself if I am following the instructions and the examples that I find in the Scriptures – which brings everything so much closer to home. During my morning Bible reading time, the Lord often gives me instructions for the day. I'm reminded to give someone a phone call or I think of something to put on my grocery list. I often get ideas for whatever project I'm working on at the time.

Another thing I do is to note down special Bible verses that I come across. I put these in a Bible memory file, and I memorize these verses as I find time.

If we read prayerfully and meditatively, God will bring us into an understanding of how to live our lives. As we read, let us remember that the Lord is the Lord. We are His servants, even bondservants, and our commitment is to obey the Master. This is what servants do.

Read Consistently

One of the great challenges of our daily walk with the Lord is to find time to spend with Him. It can be a challenge to find the time for Bible reading, study, prayer and all the rest.

It goes without saying that we need to set priorities. The temptation is to say that our time with the Lord must take top priority, no exceptions. But the reality is that life gets in the way. Please don't allow yourself to fall into a guilt trip if you genuinely can't find time.

Most of us can find time.

There are lots of good books out there on productivity and goal setting. These books may help you find time for things your need to do with limited time constraints. All of them stress the importance of a daily routine.

Set a goal for reading your Bible in, say, six months or a year, then consult one of these resources for setting up a daily strategy.

It all boils down to consistency. You can do it!

Don't Neglect the Other Aspects of Your Devotional Life

As a student of the Bible, I never want to downplay the importance of Bible study. In my own life, I do my best to find time for both reading and study.

I also make time to talk directly with the Lord through prayer and I always try to honor Him in adoration and praise.

Seek the Lord about where He wants you to focus your time with Him. Let Him take control of your daily walk with Him. He will surely lead you.

Chapter 12

How to Read a Book of History

Let's begin at the beginning, with Genesis since it's the first book of the Bible. It is classified as a history book.

History books are written in narrative (or prose) form which means these books are written pretty much like people talk. Poetry, on the other hand, is traditionally written with rhythm and rhyme, but people don't normally talk that way.

The naturalness of narrative makes for easy reading which means that we can relax and enjoy these books. And the best news is that most of the Bible is narrative.

Genesis is a great start to the Bible. It is easy to read, and it is filled with fun stories. This is true of most of the Bible's history books.

Here are some tips for reading the history books.

Don't Lose the Historical Thread

Keeping track of the historical thread is one of the main "how to" principles that I focus on in this book. It's especially important when reading the books of prophecy. For example, if you want to understand Isaiah, you'll need to understand what was going on historically and politically when he prophesied.

So, where do you get the historical context for Isaiah? You read the historical books, specifically II Kings in this case. The historical books from Genesis to Esther provide the historical context for the entire Bible.

So, don't lose the historical thread.

Get Your Children Involved

Read with special attention to stories that you can teach your children. If your children are old enough to read for themselves, pick out stories for them to read. If there is dialogue, have them create little skits or plays that they can perform at family time. Read stories aloud to the younger children. Have some of your older children read a story, and then tell it in their own words to their younger brothers and sisters.

The history books contain endless activities for children. If they are artistically inclined, have them draw a picture of David and Goliath. If they like music, have them write little songs that tell about historic events (Miriam wrote a song telling how the children of Israel were delivered from the Egyptians). Have your children build things like a replica of the ark.

The history books are a wonderful introduction for helping your children develop a love for the Bible. Use your own Bible reading to come up with terrific ideas.

But the history books were also written for *you*, not just your children. Write your own stories, draw your own pictures. Let your creative juices flow.

And never stop learning something new about the Lord.

Stay Engaged

Most of the historical books are easy to read. Some of them contain law interspersed with narrative, and that makes these books a bit harder to get through. Some history books contain genealogies which a lot of people find boring. Sometimes it's difficult to stay engaged.

I've learned to enjoy most of the history books, but things start to drag for me in parts of II Kings. The dull narrative will say something like, "So and so became king, and he reigned for *x* number of years and he did evil in the sight of the Lord and he slept with his fathers and was buried in …." The next set of verses will read, "His son so and so became king, and he reigned for *x* number of years and he did evil in the sight of the Lord and he slept with his fathers and was buried in…" and so forth.

Get through these sections as best you can but *wake up and pay attention* when you get to the final kings: Hezekiah, Manasseh,

Jehoiakim, Jehoiachin and the others. The very last king was Zedekiah who fled when Nebuchadnezzar's army overran Jerusalem. But they caught up with him and put his eyes out before they carried him off to Babylon.

The reason you need to pay attention here is because you need the historical context to understand the Babylonian captivity and the prophets, Jeremiah in particular.

Watch the Panorama of God's Plan of Salvation Unfold

As you read through the history books, pay special attention to how terribly sinful and rebellious God's children were. They'd only been out of Egypt for a few days before they started complaining. And they complained for the next 1,000 years or so.

Watch the panorama unfold. The people disobey. God shows mercy. They disobey again. He shows mercy again. He gives them the law. They disobey the law. He gives specific instructions on many occasions and they ignore all of them.

During all this time, God is planning to give us his Son to save us from our sins. In the New Testament we see the culmination of the plan of salvation, and in the last two chapters of Revelation we see John's vision of the new heaven and the new earth.

That's where we're headed!

Chapter 13

How to Read a Book of Law

Some years ago, I read a biography of India's great liberator, Mahatma Gandhi. I learned that *Gandhi-Ji*, as the Indians respectfully call him, had this to say about the Bible: "I started to read it once, but I got bored and quit."

I believe I laughed out loud! If you're a Bible reader, you'll know exactly what happened. Gandhi read all of Genesis and the first half of Exodus. Then he had to wade through the second half of Exodus. If he survived that, he got to Leviticus, and it was all over.

Leviticus is a *book of law*. It contains the ancient Jewish legal code. For most people, Gandhi included, it is the most dull and boring book ever.

I was in a lawyer's office recently and he had a set of 20 or so books on one of his shelves. It was a collection of Kansas law. I picked one volume off the shelf, looked at a few pages, and quickly put it back. Who would actually read these twenty volumes of Kansas law?

Probably nobody. It's reference material.

Leviticus isn't reference material. And it isn't just any old legal code. It is God's Word. As Bible readers, we are committed to reading the entire Bible, every word of it.

So please don't become discouraged and quit as Gandhi did. If you keep reading your Bible, the law will come alive for you at some point, and then it won't be boring at all.

Learn to Love the Law

Learn to love the books of law. One of the things that really helped me in this area was to read the testimonies of the people who really did just that: they loved the law. Psalms is a good source. In fact, the longest psalm in the Bible, Psalm 119, is almost exclusively devoted to praising the Lord for the law. Here are a few verses to encourage you.

Open my eyes, that I may see
Wondrous things from Your law. (verse 18)

Give me understanding, and I shall keep Your law;
Indeed, I shall observe it with my whole heart. (verse 34)

I shall keep Your law continually, Forever and ever. (verse 44)

I remember Your name in the night, O Lord,
And I keep Your law. (verse 55)

The law of Your mouth is better to me
Than thousands of coins of gold and silver. (verse 72)

Let Your tender mercies come to me, that I may live;
For Your law is my delight. (verse 77)

Oh, how I love Your law!
It is my meditation all the day. (verse 97)

I long for Your salvation, O Lord,
And Your law is my delight. (verse 174)

Appreciate the Social Value of the Law

When you live in a developing society, as I have, you'll see squalor and disease almost everywhere. When you read Leviticus, you'll become keenly aware that squalor and disease had no place among God's children. You'll find chapter after chapter devoted to sanitation laws and disease prevention. You'll also find property law, criminal law, tax law, marriage law and inheritance law. It's all there. God thought of everything for structuring a lifestyle and a society that would run perfectly.

Whenever I read the law I stand in awe of the loving God who so meticulously laid out the perfect standard for his children to live by!

Sit up Straight and Take Notes

With some narrative portions of the Bible you can curl up in an easy chair near the cozy fireplace and read and read. If you try that with a book of law, there's an excellent chance you'll fall asleep.

To read the books of law you'll need to sit up and pay attention. Take notes. Jot down a few comments about the various kinds of sacrifices, and the Spring and Fall festivals as you come across them. They don't have to be extensive notes. When you finish a chapter, just jot down in one or two sentences about what it said.

If you can't think of anything to say it's probably because your mind was wandering. Note taking is a wonderful tool to use against boredom, and your preliminary observations will provide an excellent springboard for further study.

Let the New Testament Come Alive

As you're taking notes, you'll notice that the New Testament becomes clearer. Did you ever wonder why Jesus told the leper he'd healed to show himself to the priest? The answer is in the law. Did you ever wonder what it meant when Paul purified himself in Acts 21? The answer is in the law. Did you ever wonder why Mary and Joseph traveled to Jerusalem after Jesus' was born? The answer is in the law. Do you know why Jesus and his family were in Jerusalem when he was twelve? The answer is in the law.

It's all there. In fact, the more clearly you understand the books of law, the more clearly you will understand the New Testament and Jesus' atoning death on the cross.

Just Read It!

There was once a time when I dreaded the dull reading of Leviticus and the other portions of the law. That day is behind me now. You may still be struggling. If nothing I've said makes you want to read the law, then just *read it whether you want to or not.*

Remember the Bible Reader's Creed:

> *With God's help, I will read my Bible,*
> *every word, in the proportion that God gave,*
> *over and over again for the rest of my life.*

You'll do well. The first few times are the hardest. After that, Exodus, Leviticus, Numbers and Deuteronomy become like old friends that you visit each time you read your Bible through.

Chapter 14

How to Read the Book of Job

If you've ever tried to read Job, you've probably wanted to give up. At least that has been my experience. In my many attempts at reading Job, I've been discouraged, frustrated and downright bored.

Believe me, I've been there with Job.

Still, Job is a part of God's Word. He expects us to read it.

In my most recent Bible read-through, I was using a plan that I found on the web. I got as far as Esther and was bracing myself for Job. But next on the reading schedule was Psalms 1:1. The plan skipped Job completely!

I don't know if it was a simple oversight or if the good folks who designed the plan left it out on purpose. Whatever the case, we're not going to skip Job! We are going to follow the Bible Reader's Creed:

> *With God's help, I will read my Bible,*
> *every word, in the proportion that God gave,*
> *over and over again for the rest of my life.*

In the opening prologue, Job, a very wealthy man, gets hit with a series of disasters. Job doesn't know why this happened, but he has three friends, Eliphaz, Bildad, and Zophar who attempt to explain why he's facing hardship. As you'll read, the three friends get it all wrong.

Read the Book in Sections

I used to get frustrated because I would read chapter after chapter of phony wisdom, and I'd get confused. I'd read something I thought was really profound, and then I would notice it was a quote from Bildad. In truth, Bildad's words were worthless.

I was frustrated because I was constantly losing track of who said what. The solution is to read Job in *sections*. When you finish a section, think about it, take notes, and then *put down your Bible until the next day.*

Here's what I mean by sections. Starting in Chapter 4, there are three rounds of dialogue:

Round 1:
- Eliphaz speaks and Job answers
- Bildad speaks and Job answers
- Zophar speaks and Job answers

Round 2:
- Eliphaz speaks and Job answers
- Bildad speaks and Job answers
- Zophar speaks and Job answers

Round 3:
- Eliphaz speaks and Job answers
- Bildad speaks and Job answers
- (Zophar doesn't speak in round 3)

I would suggest that for the first day of reading these dialogues, you limit yourself to what Eliphaz says. If you have time, you can read Job's reply. Then stop. The next day pick up with Bildad. That way you won't get confused about who said what.

Learn to Love the Book of Job!

The Bible has some difficult books, and Job is one of them. With all the difficult books in the Bible, the objective is the same: learn to love them.

When you start out, have a positive attitude, and then just get yourself through your reading assignment any way you can. Each read-through will be easier than the last.

At some point the light will shine. Reading Job will be easy, and something you look forward to. You are going to love Job!

Chapter 15

How to Read a Book of Poetry

You're in for a treat when you come to the poetic section of the Bible. I'm speaking of Job, Psalms, Proverbs, Ecclesiastes, Song of Solomon and Lamentations.

One of the things that poetry does is stir up emotions. It uses words to inspire us and awaken our deepest feelings. The poetic books of the Bible reach down into our very souls and comfort us at that level.

In reading the prophets and Paul's letters, it is extremely important not to lose the historical thread. With poetry, the background history is less important. The books of poetry seem to rise above historical circumstances.

Job

Although Job is set in poetry, it is a special case, so please read Chapter 14 entitled, "How to Read the Book of Job."

Psalms

The book of Psalms is perhaps the greatest body of poetry ever compiled. Read Psalms with a sense of wonder.

Allow yourself to be emotionally moved when you read Psalms. I remember reading the 8th Psalm when I was only about 10 years old and being deeply touched by these verses:

> *When I consider Your heavens, the work of Your fingers,*
> *The moon and the stars, which You have ordained;*
> *⁴What is man that You take thought of him,*
> *And the son of man that You care for him?*
>   *(Psalm 8:3-4 NASB)*

Even as a young child I would look at the night sky and be genuinely stirred when I thought about God's love for us.

Meditate over the Psalms. As you read through Psalms, you'll find a few favorites. Use these to meditate over during your quiet time and throughout your day.

Commit your favorite Psalms to memory. In my walk with the Lord, I've struggled with memorizing Bible verses, but I've managed far better with passages. I enjoy memorizing Psalms.

When our son Paul was eight years old, I decided to teach him the 121st Psalm, one of my favorites. He was in the process of memorizing it when the Lord suddenly took him in a tragic accident.

The last verse of Psalm 121 says:

The Lord shall preserve going out and your coming in
From this time forth, and even forevermore. (Ps 121:8)

You'll finds hundreds of memory verses and passages in Psalms.

Let the Psalms minister to your personal need. The Psalms are a perfect place to turn when you are facing a difficult situation.

Some people have wondered why the Lord didn't protect Paul as promised in the verse of the Psalm he was memorizing. I've always taken the verse to mean that Paul *was* under God's guardianship when He took him. This verse has been a great comfort to me when I think about Paul.

Teach the Psalms to your children. Children have very tender hearts, especially if you nurture that aspect of their personalities. Teach them to love the Psalms. They are not too young to be touched and moved by them, and they will grow up with a deep longing for the Lord planted in their minds.

Proverbs

The book of Proverbs can be a fascinating read. It's full of little pieces of wisdom and advice that we can pattern our lives from. There's nothing difficult in the content of Proverbs, just straightforward wisdom.

Take a few cursory notes if you wish. You might have your notebook set up in columns, one column for wisdom another column for marriage, etc. When you come to a reference that relates to marriage, jot down the reference in that column. For example:

> *Houses and riches are an inheritance from fathers*
> *But a prudent wife is from the Lord. (Prov 19:14)*

If you are pressed for time, you don't necessarily have to write out the verse, only the reference. This simple exercise keeps you alert, organizes Proverbs by subject matter, and serves as an excellent springboard when you want to study a topic further.

Commit some proverbs to memory. As you read through Proverbs, you may notice a verse that stands out. This is the cream that is rising to the surface, just for you. Jot the verse down on a flash card or copy it into your smart phone. Then throughout the day refer to this special verse and meditate on it. In time, you'll have it memorized. Here's a favorite memory passage from Proverbs.

> *Trust in the Lord with all your heart*
> *And do not lean on your own understanding;*
> *In all your ways acknowledge Him,*
> *And He shall direct your paths. (Prov 3:5-6)*

Collect a few memorized passages for life instructions. Here's one you can quote to your teenager who refuses to get out of bed in the morning.

> *As the door turns on its hinges,*
> *So does the lazy man on his bed. (Prov 26:14)*

Ecclesiastes, Song of Solomon and Lamentations

These are the remaining books of poetry. I suggest simply reading them as you would any poem. Be sure to get your emotions involved. That is the purpose of poetry. When you read Song of Solomon, get into a romantic mood and let your emotions flow. With Lamentations, grieve and cry over the suffering of Jerusalem. Put yourself in a contemplative mood when you read about futility in Ecclesiastes.

I've included more information about these books in Section 4, Chapter 24.

Chapter 16

How to Read a Book of Prophecy

In our read-through of the history books of the Old Testament we noticed that the Lord began to use prophets more and more beginning in the era of the Kings of Israel and Judah.

Simply stated a prophet is a person who speaks God's truth to the people directly, face to face. In all there are sixteen books of prophecy in the Old Testament, each book written by a different prophet.

Sometimes the Old Testament prophets spoke to crowds, sometimes to individuals. Sometimes they brought an individual or a nation to account for a specific sin. Sometimes they spoke about the future.

I've always found the prophetic books of the Bible to be a challenge. In fact, I think these books require a greater degree of formal study than the historical books, poetry books and the others. You will never come to deep understanding of the prophets until and unless you devote time to serious study.

Of course, the same can be said of every book in the Bible. To gain a deep understanding of God's Word requires study, real study, and lots of it.

But we're not doing that here. Our purpose is to pull together a panoramic view of God's message to a fallen world. In reading the prophetic books, our purpose is the same: to understand in the broadest possible sense what the individual prophets are telling us.

Once we grasp the panoramic view, *then* we can zoom in and scrutinize these books at a deeper level.

So, here are my tips for reading the prophets and getting the most out of them.

If You Don't Understand Something, Don't Fret

The prophetic books contain a bottomless depth of wisdom and knowledge. None of us understands them fully.

So ... don't fret if you don't understand much the first few times through. You are striving for an overview of the prophetic books. With each pass, you'll understand more than the last time. In depth study comes later.

Take Notes

Whenever I come across difficult books in the Bible, I find it helpful to take notes. Just read a chapter and write down a summary in a few sentences. It doesn't take much time, but it really helps pull things together.

Also, if you are reading carefully, questions will arise. Write these down, too. They are your springboards for further study.

Get a Sense of the Prophet's Heart

Isaiah's personality is quite different from Jeremiah's. A careful reading of these books will give insight into individual prophets' burdens and concerns for Israel, their frustrations with rebellious people and their devotion to God.

As you read, put every effort into understanding the heart of the prophet you're reading.

Pick out Meaningful Verses.

Some verses will pop off the page. Write these down. Memorize them if you wish. Don't worry too deeply about context at this point because some verses have stand-alone value. Take these verses as God's cream rising to the surface, just for you.

This morning I was reading Isaiah and this verse just stood out and resonated with my spirit.

The grass withers, the flower fades,
But the word of our God stands forever." (Isaiah 40:8)

Don't Lose the Historical Thread

All the prophets lived at a specific time in Jewish history. They spoke to events that were happening during their lifetimes. Don't lose track of these events.

Some of the books tell the exact timeframe. For example, we learn from Isaiah 1:1 that he prophesied during the reigns of four Kings of Judah: Uzziah, Jotham, Ahaz and Hezekiah. When you read Isaiah, keep your thumb in the book of II Kings to refresh your memory about what was going on socially and politically during the reigns of these four kings.

Discern Who the Prophet is Speaking To

Always maintain a sense of who the prophet is speaking to. The default audience tends to be general. That is, the prophet is speaking to anybody who will listen.

On occasion a prophet may have a message for a specific group of people such as when Haggai spoke to the residents of Jerusalem about finishing the temple. Sometimes the prophet speaks to an individual as Isaiah did when King Hezekiah was ill. Isaiah said,

> *Thus says the Lord, the God of David your father: I have heard your prayer, I have seen your tears; surely I will add to your days fifteen years.*   *(Isaiah 38:5)*

Always try to maintain an understanding of who the prophet is speaking to.

Discern the Time Frame of Fulfillment

In the example of God adding fifteen years to King Hezekiah's life, we immediately know the time frame of fulfillment: fifteen years. Sure enough, the Bible records that Hezekiah died exactly fifteen years later. This is an example of a short-term prophecy.

Other prophecies have an unspecified time for fulfillment, such as the coming of the Messiah. We Christians believe these prophecies were fulfilled when Jesus came. Jews are still waiting for the Messiah. In His wisdom, God chose not to reveal the date of the Messiah's coming.

As you read through, try to discern whether a prophecy has been fulfilled or not. For example, Isaiah prophesied the destruction of Damascus.

Behold, Damascus will cease from being a city,
And it will be a ruinous heap. (Isaiah 17:1)

Damascus is one of the oldest continuously inhabited cities in the world, and it's still there. This is an example of a prophecy that has not been fulfilled yet.

As you go through the prophets, give some thought about when and how the various prophecies have been or will be fulfilled.

Always Be Thinking of Jesus

The entire Old Testament points to the Lord Jesus Christ. The law and the prophets are especially rich in their foreshadowing of Him. When you come across a passage like Isaiah 53, give it deep thought and meditation.

Rejoice when you read Zechariah's words,

In that day His [Jesus'] feet will stand on the Mount of Olives, which is in front of Jerusalem on the east; and the Mount of Olives will be split in its middle from east to west by a very large valley, so that half of the mountain will move toward the north and the other half toward the south." (Zechariah 14:4 NASB)

By the way, has this prophecy been fulfilled yet? And then there's this little gem from the book of Micah:

But you, Bethlehem Ephrathah, Though you are little among the thousands of Judah, Yet out of you shall come forth to Me The One to be Ruler in Israel... (Micah 5:2)

Who was born in Bethlehem? Jesus was.

Use Outside Sources

It's helpful to do a little bit of preparation before reading the prophets. Chapters 25 and 26 in this book give introductions to each book of prophecy. These are intended to be short and concise, just little springboards to get you going.

More extensive overviews and summaries are available on the internet, in Bible dictionaries, in study editions of the Bible, and similar resources. Take advantage of these for added insight.

Chapter 17

How to Read the Gospels

Until now, we have been making our way through the Old Testament. It's been quite a journey, and not all of it easy.

We've seen how sinful the children of Israel were. Within days after their miraculous escape from Egypt, they started rebelling against the Lord. For the next thousand years they continued rebelling until the Lord finally sent them into captivity again, this time in Babylon.

During those thousand years God was preparing the way for the Messiah to come to earth to save us from our sins.

We've been waiting for the Messiah, and now, *finally*, with the opening of the New Testament, He has come!

The Good News!

The word *gospel* means "good news." The official name of the book of Matthew is *The Gospel According to Matthew*, which means "The Good News According to Matthew," or "Matthew's Account of the Good News."

The good news is simply this: the long-awaited Messiah (or Christ) has come to save us from our sins.

There were four gospel writers, Matthew, Mark, Luke and John. Each of these men took it upon himself to write down the story of the life of Jesus Christ so that we could learn about Him even 2000 years later.

The birth of Jesus is only recorded in Matthew and Luke, but all four gospels describe His three years of ministry, and all four give *heavy emphasis* on His death and resurrection.

The death and resurrection of Jesus Christ is the central component of God's entire plan of salvation. Without the death and resurrection of Jesus Christ, there is no salvation and there is no Christianity.

Involve Your Children

The gospels are written in narrative and are easy to read. They are filled with stories that children can enjoy, like the time He was baptized in the Jordan River or the time He raised Lazarus from the dead.

The gospels contain *parables*, which is the Bible term for the simple stories that Jesus told to explain a spiritual truth. The *Good Samaritan* and the *Prodigal Son* are two of His famous parables.

The gospels also talk about events in Jesus' life, such as when He was born and how He died. All these topics are suitable for children. You can read stories about Jesus aloud to your children, straight from the Bible, either at family devotion time or at bedtime. Some portions are easy enough for a 3rd or 4th grader to read on their own, so encourage them to do that.

Reach into the Deep

The gospels also contain the sermons of Jesus. The most famous of these is the Sermon on the Mount which is recorded in the book of Matthew. This sermon uses language that is so easy that almost anybody can read it. The problem is that it takes a life-time to absorb the truth presented. One of the reasons we commit ourselves to reading the Bible over and over again for the rest of our lives is simply this: with each pass, we absorb a bit more truth.

The gospels, especially the book of John, document Jesus' disputes with the religious leaders of the day. These men were so intent on destroying Jesus and His ministry that they eventually succeeded in having Him put to death. Jesus' dialogues with these men were dramatic, and full of very deep truth. You'll have to dig deep to understand what was going on.

Don't Lose the Historical Thread

As with the Old Testament, we must never lose the historical thread when reading the New Testament.

As a young adult, I used to get frustrated when I would hear a sermon about the Sower and the Seed or about the time Jesus healed the woman with the flow of blood. Sometimes I would be a part of a Bible study that picked apart Jesus' teachings on a certain topic, and again I would find myself frustrated.

Don't get me wrong. I appreciated the sermons and the Bible studies. The frustration lay in the fact that I couldn't understand the setting. At what point in His life did Jesus preach the Sermon on the Mount? What was going on in the larger context of Jesus' life and ministry when John the Baptist was beheaded?

It is difficult to understand Jesus' ministry without grasping the timeline of events in His life. So, pay attention to what is going on in the background when Jesus preaches or performs a miracle. This is one of the areas where Bible reading lays a strong foundation for Bible study.

For example, the Gospel of John tells us that at some point Jesus went to Jerusalem to attend the Feast of Tabernacles. When you read this story, ask a few simple questions. Where was Jesus travelling from when He decided to go to Jerusalem? How long did the trip take? What was the feast of Tabernacles? What time of year was it? What were the people in Jerusalem doing during the Feast of Tabernacles? Your understanding of Leviticus will help you here. Also, we know from the gospels that Jesus' ministry lasted about three years before He was crucified. At what point in those three years did this trip take place?

So, pay attention to the historical thread. It will really help you put the pieces of Jesus' life and ministry together into one beautiful tapestry.

Don't Miss the Climax

What's the main point of Jesus' life? His death and resurrection. His time here on earth has no meaning without it. Christianity has no meaning without it, and you might even argue that human existence has no meaning apart from Jesus' death and resurrection.

The gospels contain 63 chapters altogether. Of these, 31 chapters (49.2%) are devoted to Jesus' last week on earth, and 18 (28.6%) deal with His last 24 hours and His resurrection. These numbers should give us some understanding of the emphasis gospel writers placed on Jesus' death and resurrection.

Don't skim over the last chapters of the gospels. These chapters tie everything together from Genesis to Revelation.

And Here's the Best Part of All

We get to fall in love with Jesus all over again when we read the gospels.

When you read the gospels, get your emotions involved! Jesus had emotions, and you can feel them if you choose to. You can get angry when Jesus got angry and cleansed the temple. You can be moved with compassion as Jesus was when he saw the crowds and healed the sick. You can rejoice as Jesus did when God hid truth from wise people and gave it to children. You can weep when Jesus wept over the city of Jerusalem and over the death of Lazarus.

You can stir up your own emotions as well. Cheer when He raises someone from the dead. Develop a sense of wonder when you see Him walking on water and calming storms. Let yourself go. What emotions to you feel when you read about Jesus sweating drops of blood before His crucifixion?

Love is an emotional experience. When you comprehend Jesus' love for you, you'll be flooded with emotions you've never experienced before.

Getting to know Jesus and loving Him more and more is the best part of reading the gospels.

Chapter 18

How to Read the Epistles

In the first years after our Lord's ascension into heaven, Christian leaders started writing letters to one another and to churches. Bible scholars call these letters "epistles." Twenty-one of these letters have survived the centuries and are included in our New Testament. Thirteen of these were written by a man named Paul. The remaining eight were written by other church leaders in the 1st century.

Paul's Letters

Paul was a towering figure in the early history of the church. The book of Acts records his conversion, his three missionary journeys, his hearings before Felix, Festus and Agrippa, and his final journey to Rome. From chapter 9 onwards, the book of Acts is kind of a mini biography of Paul.

A careful reading of Acts will also give you a sense of Paul's personality, his ethical standards, and his burden for the churches. As you read through his letters, try to expand your understanding of his personality and character.

When you get to know Paul, you'll observe the gold standard of how Christians should live their lives. Of course, we can't hope to duplicate Paul's accomplishments, but we can strive to reach his standards of humility, his love for the Lord, his love for the people he is writing to, and his dedication to truth.

Understand the Structure of Paul's Letters

Most of Paul's letters are divided into two parts: a theological section and a practical section. Romans is a good example. Chapters 1-11 are difficult to read because of their deep theological content. Yet in the middle of all the difficult concepts we find gems like,

The just shall live by faith (Rom 1:17)

and

> *But God demonstrates His own love toward us, in that while we were still sinners, Christ died for us. (Rom 5:8)*

Then in chapter 12, Paul suddenly shifts gears and gives his readers practical advice. He talks about Christian behavior, attitudes toward government and other practical matters.

Don't Lose the Historical Thread

Also, with Paul you don't want to lose the historical thread. Be sure to have the book of Acts fresh in your mind as you read Paul. His letters are interwoven with the events in his life and journeys which are recorded in the book of Acts.

For example, we know from Acts that Paul spent three years in Ephesus. We know that there was a huge riot there, and we know that there was a heart-wrenching tearful good-bye scene when Paul told the Ephesian believers that he would never see them again.

Keep these events in your mind as you read Paul's letter to the Ephesians. Notice how deeply Paul loved this church.

Take Notes

When you read Paul's letters, don't expect to understand everything. You'll need to do an in-depth study to the get most out of them. At the same time, each read-through will give a clearer view than the last read-through. You'll know when you're ready for that in-depth study because at some point you'll develop a thirst and a longing to learn more.

In the meantime, take notes. Read a chapter and write a few sentences about its content. This exercise will give you an excellent overview of what Paul has to say, and it will also serve as a springboard for further study.

The General Epistles

The remaining letters, written by James, Peter, John and Jude, are collectively known as the general epistles. The general epistles weren't written to specific individuals or churches. They were written to the church at large, and that is why they are called *general* epistles.

With Paul's letters each book is named after the *recipient*, the letter to the Romans, to the Galatians, to Timothy, etc. With the general epistles, each book is named after its *author*.

The exception is Hebrews which was named after the recipients. No one knows who wrote Hebrews, but the letter was clearly written to the early Jewish Christians, hence the name, *Hebrews*, another name for Jews.

Read the General Epistles as You Would Any Letter from a Friend

Hebrews is the most theological of the general epistles, and therefore the most difficult to read. As you read Hebrews, take note of how Christ is superior to the angels, to Moses, and to the priesthood. Don't miss the famous chapter on faith and pay attention to the practical advice in the closing chapter.

James is full of down-to-earth guidance which will help you in your daily walk with Jesus.

Peter's two letters show us a new side of Peter's personality. In the gospels, Peter is impulsive and often a bit reckless, the kind of person who acts before he thinks. In Acts, he suddenly matures and becomes a great leader. In his letters we see that he has developed into a great teacher as well.

John's three letters, written when he was an old man, read like a loving letter from somebody's favorite grandfather. He keeps referring to us as "my little children."

And then there's *Jude*. This book is only 25 verses long. Just read it! You'll find a stern warning against false teachers. It's a warning we need to take seriously today.

Chapter 19

How to Read Revelation

I remember that when I was a little girl, I'd pick up a Bible and thumb through it looking for a Bible verse or passage. If I accidently thumbed too far to the right, I'd come to Revelation. Just seeing the word on the page caused me to break out into some kind of panic. I'd quickly close my Bible and try to wipe out thoughts of the end of the world. I'd heard it was to end by fire – and the thought terrified me.

I don't recall when I first got the nerve to read Revelation, but I can truthfully say that I have outgrown my childhood fears. Revelation not only tells us how the world will end, but it also shows us the grand finale of God's entire plan of salvation. It's all about our glorious future in heaven.

So, be sure to read Revelation! It would be a glum experience to read a really great novel – but skip the last chapter.

Two Reading Methods

There are two ways you can read Revelation. The *first* is to simply read it, and then tick it off your list and congratulate yourself for finishing the Bible. I've done that lots of times.

The *second* way is to read it with serious thought. *Take notes!*

Revelation is full of lists – the seven seals, the four horses, the seven bowls. Jot them down as you come to them, and make a note of what happens when each seal is opened, etc. Gain an overview of how everything fits together. Look at the *panorama* of the end times.

Don't Do This:

There is one thing I would suggest that you *don't* do. Please don't delve too deeply into Bible study at this point. Our purpose here is to read comprehensively and learn as much as we can in terms of overview.

Be particularly wary of trying to develop a timeline for end-time events just now. People who are interested in eschatology (the study of the end times) disagree strongly regarding when specific events will occur. Some people firmly believe than a certain event called the rapture will take place before another event called the tribulation. Other scholars believe that it will happen midway through the tribulation, or even after the tribulation. Who is right?

I've been to my share of Bible studies regarding end times, and here's what usually happens: someone who believes fervently in one of the timeline scenarios will lead you through all the passages in Revelation that support his theory. Another time a different teacher will lead you through all the passages in Revelation that support his fervent belief in the *opposite* view.

This is a backwards approach to Revelation. Before you pick passages apart, *learn what the book says!* Do your due diligence to getting the overview firmly established in your mind before you take on a detailed study. I would suggest reading the entire book of Revelation – with notes – at least ten (10) times before you even *think* about putting a timeline together.

Of course, if you read your Bible once a year, it will take 10 years to get that far. Therefore, the study of Revelation (like all Bible study) will need to be a separate activity apart from systematic Bible reading.

Revelation is an exciting book because it tells us how everything will end. After you get through the confusing prophecies, you'll come to the last two chapters of the Bible where God describes the new heaven and the new earth. What a glorious place!

I can't wait to get there.

Part IV

The Bible Book by Book

Chapter 20

Book by Book: The Pentateuch

In Part IV of this book we'll go over all sixty-six books of the Bible in an easy informative manner. The first five books of the Bible are grouped together in a classification called *The Pentateuch*, a biblical term that literally means "five books. These five books are:

- Genesis
- Exodus
- Leviticus
- Numbers
- Deuteronomy.

Some people call them the Books of Moses since they were written by Moses. Jews refer to these five books as the *Torah*.

These books are historical in nature, but they differ from other historical books in that they also contain the Old Testament legal code, which is referred to in Scripture as The Law.

In this chapter we will go over each of the five books.

Genesis and the Beginning of Everything

Genesis is hands down my favorite book of the Bible. It has simplicity and power. It's full of drama and suspense, unforgettable Bible stories and important life messages. The book of Genesis is the foundation for understanding the rest of the Bible.

The word "Genesis" means *beginning*. It starts with the creation of the universe followed by the earth with its plants and animals and the first humans, Adam and Eve. The third chapter explains how Adam and Eve fell into sin.

The rest of the Bible (all 66 books) has one central theme: God's unrelenting effort to restore a perfect relationship between Himself and mankind. You'll see the story unfold as you read the entire Bible.

Genesis continues by telling how the earth populated. But mankind was so sinful that God destroyed most of the earth in a catastrophic flood. This is the story of Noah's Ark that you learned in Sunday School.

The earth repopulates, and God chooses a special people for Himself. He calls a man named Abraham and promises to make his descendants as numerous as the stars in the sky. This is the beginning of the Jewish people. Today's Jews, every one of them, are physical descendants of Abraham.

The rest of Genesis tells about how Abraham's descendants developed into twelve tribes. In the end, all of Abraham's descendants, only 70 men plus women and children, moved to Egypt because of a terrible famine in the land of Canaan.

Enjoy Genesis! It's an easy and fun book to read with lots of fun Bible stories.

By the way, the Book of Genesis revolves around six principle men. Can you figure out who they are?

Exodus and the Tabernacle Project

After Genesis, the book of Exodus continues with more exciting stories. For whatever reason, Exodus is my daughter's favorite Bible book.

By the time Exodus opens, the children of Israel have been in Egypt for about 400 hundred years. Now they are slaves – and very poorly treated by the Egyptians.

The Lord called a man named Moses to lead the children of Israel out of Egypt and back to Canaan. The first time I read about Israel's dramatic escape from Egypt, I thought it was just about the most exciting story I'd ever read in my life.

The book is called *Exodus* because the children of Israel *exited* (that is, took their exit from) Egypt at that time.

After they escaped from Egypt they spent some time at the foot of Mount Sinai getting ready to travel to their homeland. There are two specific housekeeping items that need to be taken care of before they can set out on the journey to the Promised Land.

• They have to understand God's instructions.

• They have to build a portable tabernacle to use as a
     house of worship during their trip.

God takes Moses to the top of Mount Sinai and gives him the *Law*. *God's Law* is a concept that is central to the Bible, and we'll read a lot about it from this point onward in Scripture. Moses introduces the Law to the people when he comes down from the mountain, but the next book of the Bible, *Leviticus*, explains it in great detail.

God also gives Moses specifications for building the tabernacle, a large, portable tent which they would use for worship. For the rest of the Book of Exodus, the children of Israel are hard at work getting the tabernacle ready for the journey.

During one of my read-throughs before I had children, I became fascinated with the tabernacle. The specifications for building the tabernacle are very detailed and I thought it would be a wonderful project to build a model tabernacle someday with a son.

I took extensive notes on how such a tabernacle could be built. At the time, I didn't even have any children, but in due time, the Lord gave my husband and me a wonderful son and we named him Paul. He was my tabernacle boy.

I wanted Paul and me to have a display that included the tabernacle itself, the courtyard with its fence and models of the altar and basin. I also wanted to make a series of dolls, models of Aaron and the other priests with their priestly garments so that we could march them around from place to place according to the instructions given in the book of Numbers.

I figured that when Paul was about eight or nine he would be old enough to understand and enjoy the tabernacle project. As it turned out, we lost our beloved Paul in an accident shortly after his eighth birthday – and my dream of building a tabernacle died with him.

I thought of building a tabernacle with my daughter, Elizabeth, but it was too painful at the time. Today when I read Exodus there is something of a wistful longing that rises up in me, thinking of what might have been. So I am passing this tremendous idea along to other parents who have sons or daughters.

And as you read Exodus, remember that both the law and the tabernacle have tremendous spiritual significance. The Lord will gradually reveal these truths to you as you remain faithful in reading His Word.

Leviticus and the Foreshadowed Christ

Leviticus is perhaps the most difficult book in the Bible to read. In short, it's a *boring* book, or can be, unless you enjoy reading legal codes. An attorney friend of mine says Leviticus is his favorite book. That's an attorney for you!

For the rest of us, we need to train ourselves to love and understand legal discourses.

In truth, a proper understanding of Leviticus is crucial in understanding the rest of the Bible. For example, in Luke 2:21-24 we read that Jesus was circumcised on the 8th day, that Mary purified herself, that Mary and Joseph brought him to Jerusalem where they offered either two turtledoves or two pigeons to the Lord. Did you ever wonder why they did those things? You'll find the answer in Leviticus.

What were the disciples doing on the Day of Pentecost? True, they were busy being filled with the Holy Spirit that day. But the Bible says, "When the day of Pentecost was fully come...." indicating that something else was going on that day. Also, a huge crowd had gathered in Jerusalem for the occasion. Curious about that? You'll learn about the Jewish feasts and festivals in Leviticus.

Jesus death on the cross cannot be fully understood without a knowledge of Old Testament sacrifices. Where are these spelled out? In Leviticus.

The beauty of Leviticus is that almost everything in it foreshadows the life of Christ. I particularly love Chapter 16 which tells about the Day of Atonement and the Scape Goat which carried the sins of the people into the wilderness – never to be seen again.

Leviticus takes its name from the term *Levite*. The Levites were the descendants of Levi, one of Jacob's 12 sons, the founder of the tribe of Levi. This tribe was in charge of the priesthood, the tabernacle and everything related to enforcing the Law. The book of Leviticus was named after them.

What is the secret to reading Leviticus? For most people it takes time, and several read-throughs before it begins to make sense. When it does, you'll enjoy reading Leviticus.

Meanwhile, if you are struggling with boredom, simply make up your mind to read Leviticus from beginning to end, no matter what. It's God's Word. Get through it any way you can. Each read-through gets easier, and in time Leviticus will become precious to you.

Numbers and the Treasury of Bible Stories

One evening at a church potluck, a friend of mine commented on the book of Numbers saying, "Did you ever read such a dull book in your entire life?"

I wasn't altogether sure we were reading the same Bible. I absolutely love Numbers! To me Numbers is really exciting precisely because it *isn't* just legal code. It has a lot of fun Bible stories interspersed with the law.

- The story of the twelve spies who explored Canaan is in Numbers.

- The story of Miriam's leprosy is in Numbers.

- The story of the how the earth swallowed up Korah and his family is in Numbers.

- The story of Aaron's staff that budded is in Numbers.

- The story of the pillar of cloud by day and the pillar of cloud by night is in Numbers.

- The story of water pouring out of a rock is in Numbers.

- The story of Balaam and the talking donkey is in Numbers.

- The story of the plague of the Lord in which 24,000 people died is in Numbers.

- The story of why Moses was forbidden to enter the Promised Land is in Numbers.

Perhaps the most significant story in Numbers is when Moses

sent twelve men (one man from each tribe) to spy out the promised land. We often refer to this group as the 12 spies.

When they returned from their expedition, ten of them gave a bad report and advised Moses against trying to enter the land. It was too heavily fortified, they said.

God was so angry with this negative report that He forbade every one of the children of Israel from entering the promised land. How did He do that? By making them wander in the wilderness for *forty* years, during which time the entire generation died out. The book of Numbers covers the entire forty-year period.

By the way, two of the twelve spies return with a positive report. They were the only people who survived the forty years and entered the promised land with the younger generation. After reading Numbers, can you name them?

Numbers gets its name from the fact that Moses "numbered" the people in the first chapter. That is, He took a census. All the men who were old enough and healthy enough to go to battle, "numbered" 603,550. After that generation had died off, Moses "numbered" the people again. This time there were 601,730 soldiers.

Numbers also contains what I call "The Tabernacle Project, Part 2." In Exodus God gave instructions for building the tabernacle. In Numbers He gave instructions for moving it from place to place. Numbers contains complete instructions for take-down, transport and set-up. I wanted Paul to know these things so that he could set his tabernacle up and take it down properly.

The problem with Numbers is that it has legal code interspersed with the interesting narrative. This is disconcerting for some, but it won't be for you when you discover its treasure chest of wonderful Bible stories and fun projects for your kids.

Deuteronomy and the Most Humble Man on Earth

There are two things that stand out in my mind from the very first time I read the Bible through many years ago. The first was the awesome panorama of God's Word. The second was that I was extremely touched by the book of Deuteronomy.

The book of Deuteronomy contains Moses' final words to the

children of Israel. He had explained the Law to the people before they started their journey. Now all those people have died in the wilderness, and there is a new generation. Moses painstakingly explains the law again to the people who haven't heard it before.

In fact, the word Deuteronomy means *Second Law*, so that is how the book got its name. Of course, it is the same law as before, but the second time Moses explained it.

My mind's eye could picture the aged Moses, now 120 years old, pouring his heart out to this new generation. Moses was about to die without entering the Promised Land and he wanted to be sure the people understood God's instructions to them.

It's his last chance to teach it to them, and there is a sense of urgency as he goes over every detail with them for the last time in a series of farewell addresses.

The Bible calls Moses the humblest man on earth. His time on earth ends when he lovingly blesses each tribe, and then climbs Mount Nebo where the Lord shows him the Promised Land from a distance. Then he dies, and the Lord Himself buries Moses in an unknown place in the plain of Moab.

In the final verses of Deuteronomy, the Bible sums up the life of Moses with these words:

> *But since then there has not arisen in Israel a prophet like Moses, whom the Lord knew face to face.   (Deut 34:10)*

What a magnificent book!

Chapter 21

Book by Book:
Joshua, Judges and Ruth

The story doesn't end with Moses' death. History keeps chugging along, and, as we'll see in Joshua and Judges, God is still dealing with disobedient and rebellious children. In fact, could we say that He is still doing that in the 21st century?

Joshua and the Great Conquest

In the last chapter of Deuteronomy, the Lord takes Moses to the top of Mount Nebo, and shows him the Promised Land, which he is not allowed to enter. Moses dies on Mount Nebo, and Joshua, the son of Nun, takes over the leadership of the children of Israel. It was his job to bring them across the Jordan River into the land of Canaan – and conquer the people who lived there.

There are some fun stories in Joshua, like when over a million people crossed the Jordan River. The famous story of the Battle of Jericho is in Joshua as well.

We know from Numbers that Joshua's army consisted of 601,730 soldiers. You would think that conquering the small towns and villages of Canaan would be a simple task for such a huge army.

But no! Our God demands obedience. Israel lost a few battles when they didn't listen to His instructions. You'll read all about it in Joshua.

The first half of Joshua is about conquering the land and driving out enemies. The second half deals with dividing up the land so that each tribe had a territory to call home.

Judges and the Age of Instability

During the earliest period after the settlement of the land, Israel was ruled by "judges," There were 15 judges, all of whom are recorded in the book of Judges except for the last two, Eli and Samuel. You'll read about them in the book of I Samuel.

This period of Israel's history is characterized by instability in government. The Bible sums up the state of affairs with this statement:

> *In those days there was no king in Israel; everyone did what*
> *was right in his own eyes.*   *(Judges 17:6)*

There are some interesting stories in Judges. Have you ever heard of Samson and Delilah? Samson was one of Israel's judges. You'll read about him and his weakness for women in the book of Judges. You'll also read about Samson's superhuman strength and the secret behind it.

One of the saddest stories is about Jephthah's foolish vow. It makes me cry every time.

Then there's the most revolting story I know of in the entire Bible. It has to do with sexual abuse and gang rape. You'll recognize it when you get there. One thing about the Bible is that God doesn't hide sin as though it didn't exist.

The book of Judges is easy to read, and for the most part it is pleasant reading. That said, be prepared to encounter a certain amount of violence. In the days of Noah,

> *the wickedness of man was great in the earth, and that every*
> *intent of the thoughts of his heart was only evil continually.*
> *(Genesis 6:5)*

What was true in Noah's time was still true in the days of the judges. Things hadn't changed much.

Ruth and True Love

From Genesis until now, we've read a lot of history. Then we find a special treasure in the book of Ruth. Ruth is a short story, so perfectly written that it turned up as required reading in one of my college literature classes.

Ruth is a beautiful love story, but I won't give a synopsis here.

It's only 3-4 pages long in most Bibles, so you can just read the real thing.

In addition to the love story between Ruth and Boaz, you'll find themes of loyalty, faithfulness, honor and blessing. Don't miss the significance of the kinsman redeemer in the third chapter. As Boaz redeemed Ruth, so has the Lord Jesus Christ redeemed us.

When you read Ruth, you'll come away with a deep sense of satisfaction. You'll know you've just read some truly great literature.

Chapter 22

Book by Book: The Era of Kings

Beginning with I Samuel, the history of Israel takes a dramatic turn. Judges had ruled Israel for perhaps 350 years. Now the Era of Kings begins. Israel is about to move from the dark ages (the period of Judges) to the Golden Age (the reigns of King David and his son King Solomon).

The Era of Kings is recorded in I Samuel, II Samuel, I Kings, II Kings, I Chronicles and II Chronicles. (Please note that in this book I am using Roman Numerals to identify these books. Sometimes you'll see them written 1 Samuel, 2 Samuel, etc.)

When we refer to these books by name we call them First Samuel, Second Samuel, etc. They are not called One Samuel, Two Samuel.

I Samuel and the Kingdom of Israel

The books of First and Second Samuel are named after Samuel, the last judge of Israel. You'll read the poignant story of his birth and childhood in the opening chapters. As a small boy Samuel learned how to recognize God's voice. As a mature adult he became one of Israel's greatest leaders, unquestionably the greatest judge.

At some point during his tenure, the people started demanding a King. Under Samuel's leadership, God gave Israel its first king, a man named Saul. King Saul was a dismal failure, so God replaced him with King David. This is the same David who killed a giant with a slingshot. It's the famous story of David and Goliath, and it is found in I Samuel.

When Saul figures out that David is a threat to his authority, he tries to kill him. The rest of the book of I Samuel records the power struggle between the two men, which is very intense at times.

The Bible says that David was "a man after God's own heart." Even in the worst moments, David honors Saul as "the Lord's anointed." He never dares to bring harm to him in any way. As you read your way through this amazing book, let David's example of humility inspire you.

David and Saul don't have just each other to worry about. The major foreign power, the Philistines, are a huge threat to Israel's security. In the last chapter of the book, King Saul is killed on Mount Gilboa in a battle against the Philistines.

II Samuel and the Reign of King David

King Saul is dead, and David is now the undisputed King of Israel. The opening chapter of II Samuel tells about King David's reaction when he hears the news of Saul's death. Did he rejoice? Well, not exactly. You can read his reaction in II Samuel, chapter 1.

The book of II Samuel covers the entire reign of King David. As you read, you'll experience the highs and lows of his reign as well as the highs and lows of his emotions. David always kept his heart close to God's heart. He was sensitive at a deeply emotional level when God was grieved.

David's great sin was his affair with a married woman named Bathsheba. As a man after God's own heart, he repented deeply and profoundly, but he still paid a dreadful price for that sin.

One of David's desires was to build a temple for the Lord. The tabernacle, built in the wilderness, was now about 400 years old. You'll read about why God didn't allow him to build his dream temple.

King David was a powerful and wise leader. At the same time, he was exceptionally humble and submissive. As you read, learn everything you can about King David's walk with God. You'll be a better Christian for it.

I Kings and the Divided Kingdom

King David is a very old man now, and in the opening chapter of I Kings there is a power struggle regarding his successor. His son Solomon wins and secures the Kingdom for himself.

One of the first things Solomon did was build his father's beloved temple. When it was finished, he brought the ark into the temple – and suddenly the glory of the Lord came as a cloud and filled the temple. Can you imagine what a sight that must have been?

Solomon, like his father, was a great king. He built the temple, expanded the kingdom, accrued tremendous wealth – and a lot of wives. But most of all, Solomon was known for his great wisdom.

Sadly, the Golden Age of Israel didn't last long. There was trouble brewing in the Northern tribes. When Solomon died, these tribes (ten of them in all) broke away and formed their own kingdom with a man named Jeroboam as their King.

There were two tribes in the South (Benjamin and Judah) that remained true to Solomon's son Rehoboam, their new king.

The split was permanent. The Northern Kingdom took the name Israel, and the Southern Kingdom was known as Judah. The rest of First Kings and the entirety of Second Kings records the history of the kings of Israel and Judah, hence the name "Kings."

We see an interesting development during this period. The Lord is beginning to use *prophets* to a greater degree than before. We've seen the occasional appearance of prophets in earlier books, but from now on, prophets play a major role in Israel's history.

The prophet Elijah first makes his appearance in I Kings 17 when he raises a widow's son from the dead. In the next chapter he confronts the priests of Baal on Mount Carmel. It is one of the most famous stories in the Bible.

II Kings and the Great Decline

II Kings continues with the history of all the kings of Israel and Judah. It can be dull reading for some, but there are stories that keep the narrative alive and fascinating.

As the Bible mentions each king it declares a few facts. The Bible generally says the name of the king, whose son he was, when he began to reign, where he reigned, how long he reigned and whether he was good or evil.

As you read through the list of kings, you'll notice a steady decline in their effectiveness and their obedience to the Lord. The kingdom of Judah had a few righteous kings, but the kingdom of Israel had none. That's right, every single king who ruled over Israel did evil in the sight of the Lord.

As we have seen, God doesn't deal lightly with a sinful nation. The Northern Kingdom lasted from 796 BC (the approximate year of the split between the two kingdoms) until 555 BC, 241 years.

What happened in 555 BC? You'll read about it in II Kings, but the Bible doesn't give the date. Historians have concluded that 555 BC was the year that the Assyrian Empire swooped down and defeated the Northern Kingdom and took the *entire population* (all ten tribes) into exile.

Have you ever heard of the ten lost tribes of Israel? Yes, they got lost. To this day nobody knows what happened to them after the Assyrians took them away. Some researchers have theories but they have never been proven.

The Kingdom of Judah fared a little better. They lasted from 796 BC until 422 BC (374 years). That's when the Babylonians conquered them and took them into captivity.

With the end of II Kings, the Era of Kings is over.

I Chronicles

I Chronicles and the next book, II Chronicles, correspond to the time period of I and II Samuel, and I and II Kings, respectively. Scholars believe that these two books may have been just one book when they were written, then separated into two books later on.

Researchers believe that these books were written *after* the Israelites returned from Exile in Babylon. The author was most likely Ezra the priest, and his purpose was to encourage the returning Jews by reminding them of their great spiritual heritage.

The first nine chapters of I Chronicles, is a long genealogy, very dull reading for most people. My advice is to stick with it as best you can.

Somewhere in those nine chapters, you'll find a true gem, the Prayer of Jabez. Lots of sermons have been preached on this prayer, and one person actually wrote an entire book that was a best seller a few years ago (The book was called *The Prayer of Jabez: Breaking Through to the Blessed Life* by Bruce Wilkinson and I highly recommend it).

Can you find the prayer of Jabez without looking it up? If you diligently read through these nine chapters (and you should), you'll come across it.

The rest of I Chronicles covers the events in David's life and ends with his death.

II Chronicles

II Chronicles is a continuation of I Chronicles and originally they were the same book. It picks up with Solomon's reign, immediately after the death of King David. In the first chapter God offers to give Solomon anything he wants, and Solomon requests wisdom to lead the people.

The rest of the book tells about how Solomon built the temple, how the Northern Kingdom split away from the Southern Kingdom, and how things went on a downward spiral from there.

II Chronicles is a reprise of the historical events recorded in I and II Kings. You've read these books, but take note of how Ezra retells the story especially for the Jews returning from exile. On the one hand, he spells out with clarity where Israel and Judah went wrong. On the other hand he stresses the redemptive hope that we have in God.

Enjoy your reading adventure!

Chapter 23

Book by Book: The Babylonian Captivity

The era of Kings is over, and now the people of Judah find themselves in captivity in Babylon.

Secular history reveals that the major political powers of the day were involved in a huge conflict for control of the Middle East. The major players were the Egyptians and her allies and the Babylonians who were allied with the Medes, Persians and Scythians. Babylon won when King Nebuchadnezzar II's forces defeated Pharoah Necho and his army at the Battle of Carchemish in 605 BC.

You don't need to know the secular history unless you want to study it (which is always a good thing). You only need to know that after Babylon gained control, King Nebuchadnezzar overran Judah, destroyed Jerusalem, and carried the Jewish nation to Babylon.

This period of Jewish history is known as the Babylonian Captivity and it lasted 70 years.

The Babylonian Empire didn't fare so well after they meddled with God's people. Isaiah prophesied that Babylon would be defeated by the Medes and that it would never be inhabited again "from generation to generation."

Sure enough, in 539 BC, the Babylonian Empire was overthrown by Darius the Mede and quickly came under the leadership of King Cyrus the Great. The city has never been inhabited since that time. You can see its ruins today on the banks of the Euphrates River in modern-day Iraq.

After Cyrus takes over, he permits the Jews to go home, rebuild Jerusalem and the temple. Interestingly, Isaiah prophesied this event – and he even used Cyrus' name – about 185 years before it happened.

So that is the historical background for the next three books of the Bible.

Ezra and the Temple Project

The Biblical narrative takes up at the very end of the Babylonian captivity. The people are preparing to go home, and they are concerned about the run-down condition of the temple in Jerusalem. With Cyrus' permission, the first group of exiles return to Jerusalem and start rebuilding the temple. These events are recorded in the book of Ezra.

The temple project is halted for a while by political shenanigans, but when King Darius I assumes leadership he carries out Cyrus' policy and allows the work to resume. During his reign, the temple is finished and the Jews celebrate the Passover for the first time in 70 years.

During this time Ezra was still in Babylon, along with many other Jews. King Artaxerxes I comes to power and appoints Ezra, a man "skilled in the law of Moses" to return to Jerusalem to be the Spiritual leader. The rest of the book describes how he set up the temple service and dealt with some important social issues.

Nehemiah, the Grieving Cup Bearer

Nehemiah's story begins in the twentieth year of the reign of King Artaxerxes I of Persia. Nehemiah was the king's cupbearer which was a high position in the service of the King. One day Nehemiah requested a favor of the king, which was to return to Jerusalem to rebuild the wall. The King gave him permission and also made him the Governor of Judea.

Nehemiah and Ezra both return to Jerusalem with the second group of exiles that returned to Jerusalem. Ezra was the Spiritual leader, and Nehemiah was the political leader (governor) of the returned Jews.

The book of Nehemiah recounts how the wall was rebuilt with its twelve gates. Of course, as things tend to go in life, there was opposition. A local political leader named Sanballat tried to stop the work. He failed, and the wall was built.

The book ends with the dedication of the wall, a renewal of the Mosaic covenant and the celebration of the feast of Tabernacles.

Judah was on its way to becoming a great nation again.

You'll enjoy Nehemiah. Pay close attention to the spiritual significance of each of the gates and rejoice when the Jews renew their covenant with the Lord.

Esther, the Queen who Saved the Jews from Destruction

For whatever reason, Esther is the only book in the Bible that does not mention God (you need to know this curious fact when you play Bible trivia games).

Though not mentioned by name, God's hand is unmistakable in the events that unfold in this amazing book.

Esther, a beautiful Jewish woman, became Queen when she married King Ahasuerus. Shortly after, the Jews came under an intense threat when a man named Haman decided the Jews should be wiped out as a nation.

Haman was the Hitler of the day, absolutely committed to killing all Jews. Queen Esther learns of the plot, tells the King – and saves the Jews.

Like Ruth, the book of Esther is easy to read. It's a riveting and spellbinding story of how she married King Ahasuerus, and how Haman's his evil scheme was thwarted. I love the book of Esther!

By way of note, most scholars believe that Ahasuerus was actually King Xerxes I who ruled Persia from 486-465 BC. King Artaxerxes I (mentioned in Ezra and Nehemiah) was his son. This would place Esther before Ezra and Nehemiah in the historical timeline of the captivity.

Chapter 24

Book by Book: Poetry

At the end of the book of Esther we have finished nearly half of the Bible, and we have completed the narrative, or historical, books of the Old Testament. The rest of the Old Testament is composed of poetry books and prophesy books.

The poetry books are Job, Psalms, Proverbs, Ecclesiastes, Song of Solomon, and Lamentations. These books were originally set to poetry in the original Hebrew. Although we have lost rhyme and rhythm in translation, the books still read like the great poetical works that they are.

Job and the Mystery of Suffering

Job is widely considered to be the first book to be written in the Bible but nobody knows for sure when the book was written or who wrote it. Bible scholars have come up with some theories which you can research when you have time.

In the opening prologue, Job, a very wealthy man, gets hit with a series of disasters. His wealth evaporates into nothing, he loses his 10 children, and he is stricken with a skin disorder that leaves him in constant pain. The only family member left is his wife who tells him to "curse God and die."

The theme of the entire book is "Why did Job suffer?" As readers, we know the answer because God explains it to us in chapters 1 and 2. But Job doesn't know what happened, and neither does anyone else.

Job has three friends, Eliphaz, Bildad, and Zophar, who try to help him understand his misfortune. They tell Job he must have done something terrible to deserve his fate. They don't know what he did, but they insist that he must have done *something*.

Job's conscience tells him he hadn't done anything wrong. And so the arguing begins.

Job's friends accuse him of this and that, and Job defends himself. They go back and forth for most of the book. Then a youthful upstart named Elihu rattles on for six chapters about how wrong everybody is.

The Lord stops the arguing when He speaks to Job from a whirlwind. You can read the rest, including how God restores Job's wealth to double what it was.

Job can be a difficult read. Please refer to chapter 12, "How to Read Job," for my best tips for getting the most out of this book.

Psalms, the Highest Form of Praise and Worship

Now we come to Psalms, the greatest body of poetry in all of world literature. If you love poetry, and you love the Lord, then Psalms is where it's at.

There are 150 chapters in Psalms, meaning there are 150 poems that can be read independently of one another. There is no "historical flow" so you don't have to read Psalm 1 before you read Psalm 2, etc.

Many people assume that since Psalms has the most chapters, it must be the longest book in the Bible. Not so. In word count Jeremiah is the longest followed by Genesis. Psalms is actually the 3rd longest book in the Bible.

The word *psalm* means "sacred song or hymn." The Psalms were poems set to music and meant to be sung. In that sense they were the earliest collection of praise and worship songs.

But there is more than praise and worship in the Psalms. As you read through them, you will notice the expression of the widest possible range of human emotions. Everything is there, joy, sorrow, anger, hope, despair.

There are questions:

> *Why do the heathen rage?*
> *And the people imagine a vain thing? (Ps 2:1)*

My God, my God, why hast thou forsaken me?
(Ps 22:1)

You'll find Psalms of thanksgiving:

O give thanks unto the Lord, for he is good:
for his mercy endureth for ever. (Ps 107:1)

You'll find deep meditative prayers:

Search me, O God, and know my heart:
try me, and know my thoughts:
And see if there be any wicked way in me,
and lead me in the way everlasting.
(Ps 139:23-24)

You'll find David's repentance after he sinned with Bathsheba:

Against thee, thee only, have I sinned,
and done this evil in thy sight (Ps 51:4)

There are songs of remorse:

By the rivers of Babylon, there we sat down, yea,
we wept, when we remembered Zion. (Ps 137:1)

There are lots of praise songs:

O praise the Lord, all ye nations: praise him, all
ye people. (Ps 117:1)

While I live will I praise the Lord: I will sing
praises unto my God while I have any being.
(Ps 146:2)

Let every thing that hath breath praise the Lord.
Praise ye the Lord (Ps 150:6)

And worship songs:

O come, let us worship and bow down: let us
kneel before the Lord our maker. (Ps 95:6)

O worship the Lord in the beauty of holiness:
fear before him, all the earth. (Ps 96:9)

Some psalms magnify the Lord

> *O Lord, our Lord, how excellent is thy name in all*
> *the earth! (Ps 8:1)*

Some psalms are instructional. They teach us how to live:

> *Blessed is the man that walketh not in the counsel*
> *of the ungodly, nor standeth in the way of sinners,*
> *nor sitteth in the seat of the scornful.*
> *But his delight is in the law of the Lord; and in his*
> *law doth he meditate day and night. (Ps 1:1-2)*

You'll notice that I have quoted from the King James Version here. I love the poetry, and it sounds so much more elegant and pleasing to the ear in the King James Version. Feel free to use an accurate modern translation if you prefer.

I'd like to make a special note of Psalms 119, a very special Psalm indeed. The whole Psalm is a tribute to the Law of Moses. It is the longest Psalm, and at 176 verses it is also the longest chapter in the Bible.

Psalm 119 is written in *acrostic* form, based on the 22 letters in the Hebrew alphabet. It is divided into 22 sections of 8 lines each. The first 8 lines all begin with the first letter of the Hebrew alphabet, a*leph*. The next group of eight lines begins the second letter of the Hebrew alphabet, b*et*. This pattern continues through the entire Hebrew alphabet – and that's how we come to 176 verses.

Depending on the edition of the Bible you are using, the 22 sections may be labeled with the corresponding Hebrew letters.

I once met a girl in India who had memorized the entire 119th Psalm in King James English. She was only about 10 or 12 at the time. Amazing!

Learn to love the Psalms. I have a few tips for reading them in the chapter "How to Read a Book of Poetry."

Proverbs

In English we have a few proverbs that most people know. "An apple a day keeps the doctor away" is one, attributed to Benjamin Franklin.

"Too many cooks spoil the broth" is another.

Here's how dictionary.com defines the word *proverb*:

"a short popular saying, usually of unknown and ancient origin, that expresses effectively some commonplace truth or useful thought."

So, as you might have guessed, the book of Proverbs is a book filled with, well, *proverbs*. Most of them were written during the era of Kings by several people, notably King Solomon.

One of the main themes of Proverbs is *wisdom*, where it comes from and how to attain it. Proverbs consistently contrasts the wise man and the fool.

He who walks with wise men will be wise, But the companion of fools will be destroyed.
(Prov 13:20)

A wise man fears and departs from evil, But a fool rages and is self-confident. (Prov 14:16)

Another contrast is between productive people and lazy people.

As a door turns on its hinges,
So does the lazy man on his bed. (Prov 26:14)

Go to the ant, you sluggard!
Consider her ways and be wise, (Prov 6:6)

Proverbs are fun, and sometimes amusing to read. They are loaded with wisdom!

God bless you as you read your way through them.

Ecclesiastes

Ecclesiastes was most likely written in the 3rd century BC. Some consider its author to be King Solomon, but the latest Bible scholars attribute it to an anonymous teacher. In English we call the book Ecclesiastes for historical reasons. Other languages (such as German) call this book, "The Preacher."

The book opens with this statement:

> *Vanity of vanities, says the Preacher,*
> *vanity of vanities! All is vanity. (Eccl 1:2)*

By using the word *vanity*, the preacher is referring to the futility and emptiness around us. The actual Hebrew word means "vapor."

When you think about it, life is pretty empty, especially if you don't know the Lord. This is the problem that the preacher addresses in Ecclesiastes. Here is how he sums it up at the end of the book.

> *Let us hear the conclusion of the whole matter:*
> *Fear God and keep his commandments: for this is*
> *the whole duty of man. (Eccl 12:13 ESV)*

So that pretty much says it all: life is empty until you find your destiny with the Lord. We are told to keep His commandments.

About 300 years later in history, the Lord Jesus Christ arrives and gives us the rest of the story. Life isn't futile after all. We have salvation in Him.

Ecclesiastes can be a difficult read. Simply do your best!

Song of Solomon

The opening verse of the Song of Solomon says, "The song of songs, which is Solomon's," indicating that the book was written by King Solomon. Scholars have debated this, and in your further study of this wonderful book, you can delve into authorship.

The date of writing is also in question. However, like other poetry books it is possible to read and appreciate the Song of Solomon without delving into the history of the period. We won't worry about dating the book, but this is something you can check out if you wish.

On its surface, Song of Solomon is a love story between a Shulamite woman and a man simply identified as her "beloved" or "the one whom I soul loves." Some interpreters believe this love story symbolizes the love between Christ and the church.

No doubt they are right about that at a deeper level of interpretation, but we can also learn a great deal from the surface message

Song of Solomon is a story of pure love between a man and a woman including the longing they have for each other when they are apart, their anticipation when they are about to meet, and their complete delight when they are together. It does not ignore the sexual component of pure love.

The Shulamite's opening statement is:

> *Let him kiss me with the kisses of his mouth.*
> *(Song 1:2)*

The Shulamite and her beloved meet a total of five times. As you read, try to discern where these divisions are. Also notice the progression of the Shulamite's thoughts.

The first time they meet, she is hesitant and self-conscious.

> *Do not look upon me, because I am dark,*
> *Because the sun has tanned me. (Song 1:6)*

The last time they meet she exudes self-confidence and says:

> *Set me as a seal upon your heart (Song 8:6)*

The Song of Solomon is all about the love relationship between a man and the woman he loves. We can learn a lot about love, purity and marriage from this book.

Song of Solomon is written in beautiful poetry. As you prepare to read it, get yourself in a nice poetic, romantic mood, and let the book come alive for you.

Lamentations

The city of Jerusalem fell to the Babylonians in the year 586 BC. Lamentations is a series of five laments over Jerusalem after the fall. It has five chapters, and each chapter contains one lament (a *lament* is an expression of grief or sorrow).

The author of Lamentations was Jeremiah according to strong tradition through the years. Lately, scholars have challenged this idea, but you are welcome to do your own research.

124 The Bible Reading Revolution

Lamentations has an interesting literary form. Like the 119th Psalm, it is an acrostic of the Hebrew alphabet. The Hebrew alphabet has 22 letters (aleph, bet, gimmel, plus nineteen more). In Chapter 1, the first word of verse 1 starts with aleph, the first word of verse 2 starts with bet, and so forth. Accordingly, chapter 1 has 22 verses.

Chapter 2 follows the exact same pattern, but in chapter 3, the first words of the first *three* verses start with aleph, the first words of the next three verses start with bet. This chapter has 66 verses.

Chapter 4 follows the same pattern as Chapters 1 and 2. The last chapter (chapter 5) is not an acrostic, but it does have 22 verses.

The acrostics are lost in translation which is sad. But it is nice to know how much thought the author put into composing these five laments.

As you read through Lamentations, think of the suffering the people of Jerusalem were going through. The fall of Jerusalem was preceded by a two-year siege which no doubt caused hunger and starvation. After the fall, the city was plundered and razed to the ground. The temple was destroyed. The people were deported to Babylon.

In addition to all of this, the people were aware of their own guilt in the matter. They had been unfaithful to God. This was their reward.

Read Lamentations and let your soul weep. Allow yourself to get caught up in the same grief and sorrow that the author was expressing as he wrote this extraordinary book. Let your imagination take you back to such a time of suffering, and the book will come alive.

Chapter 25

Book by Book: The Major Prophets

There are four major prophets in the Bible: Isaiah, Jeremiah, Ezekiel and Daniel. The first thing you will notice as you read them through is that you don't understand much. At least, that was my experience.

You'll discover, as I have, that a thorough understanding of the prophets requires a rather deep dig into serious Bible study.

We are not doing that here. We are reading the prophets in order to get a foundational overview of what they are saying. In so doing, we may not understand everything to our satisfaction, but we can certainly learn a great deal. And with each read-through, we'll learn a great deal more than we did the last time.

No doubt, you'll want to delve into a deep study of the prophets at some time in the future, and I urge you to do that.

Isaiah

Isaiah was the first, chronologically, of the four major prophets. From Isaiah 1:1 we learn that Isaiah was prophesying during the time of King Uzziah and the next three Kings of Judah, Jotham, Ahaz, and Hezekiah.

Isaiah is considered by some to the greatest of all the prophets. This of course is a subjective opinion, but not without merit. While we don't know much the prophet himself, we see how eloquent he is in his descriptions of the Living God, whom he refers to as "The Holy One of Israel." God is kind and compassionate and he has plans for the salvation of Israel which Isaiah lays out in his prophecies.

During Isaiah's time the major foreign power was Assyria. He was an active prophet in Jerusalem when Assyria conquered the Northern Kingdom and took its ten tribes into exile. This was in the sixth year of Hezekiah's reign.

After conquering the Northern Kingdom, King Sennacherib of Assyria surrounded Jerusalem with an army of 185,000 men. There would have been an enormous slaughter except that Isaiah came forth with this prophecy that encouraged the people of Judah.

> *Therefore, thus says the Lord concerning the king of Assyria:*
> *He shall not come into this city,*
> *Nor shoot an arrow there,*
> *Nor come before it with shield,*
> *Nor build a siege mound against it.*
> *By the way that he came,*
> *By the same shall he return;*
> *And he shall not come into this city,' Says the LORD.*
> *For I will defend this city, to save it*
> *For My own sake and for My servant David's sake*
> *(Isaiah 37:33-35)*

That night an angel of the Lord killed *the entire Assyrian army* and the Southern Kingdom was saved from destruction by the Assyrian Empire.

But God wasn't finished with Judah yet. Just two chapters later, Isaiah tells King Hezekiah that the Southern Kingdom will be conquered by the Babylonians, not the Assyrians. True to the Word of the Lord, Jerusalem fell to Babylon a little more than 100 years later.

Isaiah is roughly divided into two major sections. The first section is all about doom and gloom followed by a narrative section that parallels passages in II Kings. Then suddenly the book changes tone entirely and looks to our glorious future with the new heaven and the new earth. As you read through Isaiah, try to find the chapter where this sudden shift takes place.

And don't miss chapter 53. It's a prophecy about our Lord, Jesus Christ, one of the most loved passages in all of Scripture.

You're going to love Isaiah!

Jeremiah

Jeremiah's ministry begins during the reign of Josiah and continues through the turbulent years following his death. During this time Assyria was less of a threat than during Isaiah's time, but Egypt and Babylon were in a serious battle for control over the land occupied by Judah. Jeremiah was prophesying from Jerusalem which was caught in the cross-fire.

In some ways, Jeremiah seems to be the most personal of the major prophets. That is, we learn of his personal emotions and struggles during the turmoil.

Jeremiah was arrested, put in stocks, and then thrown into a dungeon where he "sank into the mud." His warnings were ignored, his writings burned, and he was carried off to Egypt against his will. The death and destruction during his lifetime would be so severe that the Lord told Jeremiah not to marry and have children.

Jeremiah prophesies the destruction of Jerusalem and counsels the people to go into exile in Babylon, and not to count on Egypt for rescue. But what do the people do? They go to Egypt to escape the Babylonians. Bad choice.

In the midst of the turbulence, Jeremiah prophesies a time of restoration and a bright future. One of the most important prophecies in the entire Bible is found in Jeremiah, chapter 31.

> *Behold, the days are coming, declares the Lord, when I will make a new covenant with the house of Israel and the house of Judah. (Jer 31:31)*

This covenant won't be like the Old Covenant which Moses copied down on stones. Jeremiah says:

> *But this is the covenant that I will make with the house of Israel after those days, says the Lord: I will put My law in their minds, and write it on their hearts; and I will be their God, and they shall be My people. (Jer 31:33)*

We Christians believe that the New Covenant was fulfilled with the coming of our Lord Jesus Christ and that Jesus Himself was the sacrificial lamb that sealed the covenant.

Jeremiah is filled with raw emotion. Let yourself get caught up in it as you read.

Ezekiel

Ezekiel, like Jeremiah, began to prophecy before the fall of Jerusalem. He is unique among prophets in that he was a priest in addition to being a prophet.

In Jeremiah, we learn that people put their trust in Egypt for deliverance from Babylon. In Ezekiel, they were putting their trust in the temple. Surely God wouldn't destroy Jerusalem and the temple where God Himself lived.

Wrong! People throughout history have misplaced their trust. Our trust is with the Lord, not the Egyptians, or even the temple of God.

In chapter 8, God shows Ezekiel what was going on inside the temple. There were 25 men standing with their backs to the temple and bowing down to the rising sun in the east. This is clearly an abomination to the Lord, so He arranges for the Babylonians to destroy the temple.

The book of Ezekiel is particularly hard on the house of Judah. In chapter 23 God compares Judah with her evil sister Israel who lusted after the gods of the Assyrians. The Lord makes it clear that He despises any form of idolatry (which He equates to prostitution) and Judah is by far the greater sinner.

Both Jeremiah and Ezekiel were carried into exile, Ezekiel to Babylon and Jeremiah to Egypt. They both died in these countries and never saw their homeland again.

Daniel

The book of Daniel is a fun book to read. The first half is filled with the stories you remember from Sunday school: King Nebuchadnezzar's golden image, the fiery furnace, Daniel and the lion's den, Belshazzar's feast where God's fingers wrote a message on the wall...

All of the stories take place during the Babylonian Captivity. In the opening chapter, King Nebuchadnezzar instructs his people to take some young men from the Hebrew exiles and bring them into his service. Daniel and three others were chosen.

Daniel is a good book for your children. Give your 4th graders a modern translation and let them sit in front of the fireplace and read away. They won't be bored. For younger children, read stories from the book of Daniel to them at bedtime.

The second half of Daniel goes into prophecy of the future. Together with the books of Zechariah and Revelation, Daniel gives a vivid image of the end times. Eschatologists (those Bible scholars who focus on how the world will end) love Daniel because it chronicles end-time events and looks forward to the time when Christ will reign eternally.

Enjoy Daniel! And don't forget to introduce this extraordinary book to your children, your grandchildren and all the neighborhood kids.

Chapter 26

Book by Book: The Minor Prophets

Now we come to the last portion of the Old Testament, a group of twelve books referred to as the minor prophets. They are called minor prophets, not because they are less important than the major prophets, Isaiah, Jeremiah, Ezekiel and Daniel, but simply because they are considerably shorter. Most of them can be read in a single sitting.

The minor prophets prophesied in roughly three time periods: Hosea, Joel, Amos, Micah and Jonah lived and worked before the fall of the Northern Kingdom in 722 BC. Nahum, Zephaniah and Habakkuk prophesied before the Babylonian captivity. The last three, Haggai, Zechariah and Malachi were written after the people returned from the Babylonian captivity. The dates for Obadiah are less certain.

We know very little about the identities of these prophets other than their names. Yet we know that they were solid men of God who gave the Word of God to us so that we could understand Him so much better, even thousands of years later.

As you read, you'll come to love these wonderful books that close out the Old Testament.

Hosea

Hosea prophesied during the reign of Jeroboam II, King of Israel. The corresponding kings of Judah were Uzziah, Jotham, Ahaz and Hezekiah. This places Hosea in the exact period as Isaiah. One major difference is that Hosea prophesied almost exclusively to the Northern Kingdom of Israel while Isaiah concentrated mostly on the Southern Kingdom, Judah.

Hosea was told by the Lord to marry a lady named Gomer who was a prostitute. She gave him three children whose names have prophetic meanings. After that, she wandered back into prostitution and he had to redeem her. That is, he actually paid money to her pimps to get her back.

One thing to note throughout the Scriptures is how much God hates both adultery and idolatry – and I mean He *really despises* them. Hosea, perhaps more than any other book, focuses on this hatred.

The entire book shows the symbolic equivalent between adultery and idolatry. The adulterous Gomer is equal to the idolatrous kingdom of Israel.

One of the things that concerns me in today's society is the rampant level of adultery, fornication, homosexuality and other sexual sins. People live together freely without marriage and homosexuals are increasingly granted recognition. People marry and divorce almost randomly it seems.

In the Bible *all* sexual sin is seen in God's eyes as idolatry against Himself. Read your Bible and you will see how deeply sexual misconduct angers Him. Consistently throughout the Word, God gives stern warnings which we need to take heed of.

But the book of Hosea is not merely a well-deserved rebuke against sin. Ultimately it is the profound story of the redemptive power of the Lord Jesus Christ. The adulterous Gomer is a symbol of the idolatrous kingdom of Israel, but as you read, notice how profoundly Hosea loved her.

Hosea married her even though she was a known prostitute. When she left he tracked her down, paid money to redeem her, and he forgave her completely. The book of Hosea is all about redemption and forgiveness.

Read Hosea and heed its warnings. Then also grasp the length and breadth of God's forgiveness for us when we repent from our sins.

Joel

Joel is a wonderful little book, only three chapters long. We don't know much about the prophet or when and where he prophesied, but we have the entire content of his writings before us.

One of the most famous verses in Joel prophesies the outpouring of the Holy Spirit, which happened on the Day of Pentecost. Peter, in his sermon that day, quoted Joel.

> *And it shall come to pass afterward That I will pour out My Spirit on all flesh; Your sons and your daughters shall prophesy, Your old men shall dream dreams, Your young men shall see visions.*   *(Joel 2:28)*

Much of the book of Joel focuses on a concept called "The Day of the Lord." He introduces it with these words:

> *Alas for the day!*
> *For the day of the Lord is near,*
> *And it will come as destruction from the Almighty.*
>   *(Joel 1:15)*

This verse is almost a direct quote from Isaiah who introduced the concept in Isaiah 13:6.

> *Wail, for the day of the Lord is near!*
> *It will come as destruction from the Almighty. (Isa 13:6)*

Joel further describes it as a great and terrible day.

So what is the Day of the Lord? It is a day of judgment which will bring both doom to the wicked and deliverance to the faithful. In the New Testament the Day of the Lord is associated with Jesus' second coming when He will descend to earth to judge the living and the dead. The earth and all wickedness will be destroyed on that day, but the new heaven and the new earth will come into existence. Then we Christians will be forever with the Lord.

The book of Joel starts off with the description of a devastating scourge of locusts and ends with the promise that Judah will be inhabited forever.

Such an amazing and encouraging little gem!

Amos

Like Hosea, Amos prophesied during the reign of Jeroboam II, King of Israel. Amos wrote during the reign of Uzziah, King of Judah, which places him in the earliest timeframe of his contemporary prophets, Hosea and Isaiah and Micah. In fact many scholars believe Amos was the first prophecy book written.

Amos wrote during a period of peace and prosperity. Both Jeroboam and Uzziah had long reigns and the serious threat from Assyria came a bit later in history. But peacetime merely served to increase complacency, and in turn the level of corruption increased.

Amos was sent by God to bring the Northern Kingdom to repentance. He specifically prophesied that the house of Jeroboam would die by the sword and that Israel would go into exile – a prophecy that angered Amaziah the priest who sent him back home. You can read about this confrontation when you get to chapter seven.

Amos wasn't a prophet by profession. He was a shepherd who also tended sycamore fruit trees, but the Lord called him anyway. Though people didn't recognize him as a prophet, he was faithful to the Lord and proclaimed a message of justice, righteousness and divine retribution for sin.

Enjoy the book of Amos!

Obadiah

Obadiah is the shortest book in the Old Testament, only one chapter long. You can read this book in 5 minutes or so.

The entire book is prophecy against Edom, a country located south and west of the Dead Sea. Edom means "red," and it was named after Jacob's red-headed twin brother Esau. The Edomites were the descendants of Esau.

If you'll remember from Genesis, there was "bad blood" between Jacob and Esau. They were constantly feuding over one thing or another, but God's blessing went to Jacob. Now, about 1,400 years later, the descendants of these twin brothers still bitterly hate each other.

And God wasn't so fond of the Edomites either. Many of the prophets spoke judgments against Edom, and Obadiah said,

Behold, I will make you small among the nations;
You shall be greatly despised. (verse 2)

Obadiah is a quick and easy read. Take the time to meditate over Edom's sins and compare them with what you see in today's world.

Jonah

It's the story of Jonah and the whale that you remember from Sunday School, except that the Bible doesn't mention a whale. It says that Jonah was swallowed by a "great fish."

Jonah was the son of Amittai according to Jonah 1:1. We know from II Kings 14:25 that he was from Gath-Hephar, a town in the Northern Kingdom, and that he prophesied during the reign of Jeroboam II, King of Israel.

The most interesting feature of Jonah is that it is all about bringing the city of Nineveh to repentance. Nineveh was the capitol of the Assyrian empire which was Israel's greatest enemy at the time. In all the other prophets, the Lord pronounces doom and destruction on Israel's enemies, but in Jonah He extends mercy to Nineveh. In this sense the book of Jonah foreshadows the era when the Lord will bring people from all nations to Himself.

God loves us all! He wants all humanity to repent and be restored to fellowship with Him!

The book of Jonah is easy enough that school age children can read it directly from the Bible. Have your children do that (they'll enjoy the story of Jonah and the big fish!), and then talk to them about Jonah's behavior and God's love for everybody.

Micah

Micah was from a small agricultural town in Southern Judah and he prophesied during the reigns of Jotham, Ahaz and Hezekiah. Isaiah was prophesying at roughly the same time in Jerusalem, but it is thought that Micah spent most of his time in the rural areas.

Micah, more than any other of the minor prophets speaks to the problem of social injustice. Rulers and rich people were constantly cheating the poor, mistreating women and children, demanding bribes, driving people from their homes, and so forth.

In this, Micah – and also Isaiah – had a positive influence on King Hezekiah who instituted significant reforms in the southern kingdom.

Micah sums up the solution for social problems with this famous verse:

And what does the Lord require of you
But to do justly, To love mercy,
And to walk humbly with your God?   (Micah 6:8)

Another thing that Micah is famous for is that he prophesied where the Messiah would be born.

But you, Bethlehem Ephrathah,
Though you are little among the thousands of Judah,
Yet out of you shall come forth to Me
The One to be Ruler in Israel,
Whose goings forth are from of old, From everlasting.
(Micah 5:2)

When the wise men from the East came to worship the baby Jesus, they first consulted King Herod about where to find Him. Herod didn't know, so he asked the chief priests and scribes where the Messiah would be born. These scholars looked in the book of Micah and told Herod to have the wise men look for Him in Bethlehem.

As always, take casual notes as you read Micah. It will help open up the message for you.

Nahum

Like the book of Jonah, this book focuses on the city of Nineveh, but it was written about 100 years later.

Nineveh was the capitol of the Assyrian Empire, known for extreme cruelty against the people of the nations it conquered. When Jonah preached in the city, the Ninevites repented of their sins and God spared them from the destruction that Jonah prophesied.

Now, one hundred years later, two things have happened. First, the Assyrian Empire has backslidden into its cruel ways. Second, the Assyrians have conquered the Northern Kingdom and taken the ten tribes of Israel into exile, never to be heard from again.

Neither of these developments pleased the Lord, so he sent the prophet Nahum to declare Nineveh's destruction. This time there was no repentance and no reprieve. The city of Nineveh fell in the year 612 BC to a coalition of the Babylonians and other powers of the day, marking the end of the Assyrian Empire.

The destruction was complete. You can see the ruins of Nineveh today in modern day Iraq near the city of Mosul.

I'm told that this little gem is a literary masterpiece in the original Hebrew using a variety of poetic forms. These are lost in translation, but the message remains along with a certain degree of elegant beauty.

Habakkuk

We know nothing about the prophet Habakkuk other than what we can deduce from this prophetic book. From the context we believe that Habakkuk wrote this prophecy sometime after Nineveh fell to Babylon in 612 BC. A few years later (605 BC) King Nebuchadnezzar defeated the Egyptians at the Battle of Carchemish, leaving Babylon as the undisputed political power in the region.

At the time of this prophecy, Judah was in an extremely vulnerable position. There was no doubt that Babylon would invade Judah, and very soon.

The book of Habakkuk is unique in that it is not addressed to Judah, Israel or any other nation. Rather, the entire book is a dialogue between Habakkuk and God. Habakkuk knows very well that judgment is coming against rebellious Judah, but why would judgment come from such a heathen source as the Baylonians?

When you read God's answer, you will see that He has everything under control. Habakkuk is satisfied in the end.

The third chapter is Habakkuk's amazing prayer of praise and adoration. It culminates with a very famous verse:

> *The Lord God is my strength, and he will make my feet like hinds' feet, and he will make me to walk upon mine high places.*
> *(Hab 3:19 KJV)*

Tucked away in Chapter 2 is another famous verse.

> *... but the just shall live by his faith. (Hab 2:4b)*

This spiritual truth forms the foundation for Paul's theology of salvation, and he quoted this verse in Romans 1:17. Later on in church history, Martin Luther used the same concept as the theological foundation for his 95 Theses. This in turn precipitated the Protestant reformation.

Among the minor prophets, Habakkuk is one of the easier books to read. Bible readers everywhere love Habakkuk!

Zephaniah

After Habakkuk provides a brief pause from doom and gloom, we jump back into it with Zephaniah, chapter one. He prophesies that the Lord will destroy *everything*, men and animals and birds and fish, literally everything! But, you ask, back in Noah's day, didn't God promise not to destroy the earth again? Well, if you read Genesis 9 carefully, you'll note that God only promised not to destroy the earth by *flood*.

So here we have it. God absolutely will destroy everything at some point in the future. The general consensus is that He will use fire next time. That's not hard to imagine in our day when a series of nuclear bombs could pretty well burn everything up in just one day.

Zephaniah also speaks about "The Day of the Lord," which was the main theme of the book of Joel. By the way, the concept of "The Day of the Lord" is an excellent topic for further Bible study. We generally associate it with the second coming of Christ, but what else is involved?

Zephaniah ends with an amazing prophecy of our glorious future after evil has been dealt with on the Day of the Lord. When you read this portion, make a list of all the wonderful things Zephaniah says we can look forward to in our glorious future with the Lord.

Haggai

Haggai is a fun book to read because it is short and sweet, and the content isn't very difficult, We have come now to the last three of the minor prophets, and it so happens that these last three prophesied *after* the Babylonian captivity. The Jews are now back in Jerusalem, rebuilding their lives.

If you will remember, Ezra returned from captivity and started rebuilding Solomon's temple which Nebuchadnezzar had destroyed. The project stopped for a while because of local opposition, and the people started working on rebuilding their homes instead.

Haggai's prophesy is all about finishing the temple. "Consider your ways" he says, because people were are busy with their own homes instead of tending to the temple. This is what has caused a drought in the land.

For once, the people listened to the prophet, and started working on the temple immediately.

Haggai is unique in that it is precisely dated. The opening verse says,

In the second year of King Darius, in the sixth month, on the first day of the month, the word of the Lord came by Haggai the prophet... *(Hag 1:1)*

Historians are very confident that the second year of King Darius was 520 BC. Scholars familiar with the Hebrew calendar date the sixth month and first day to August 29.

Haggai gave four prophecies, one on August 29, one on the second on October 17th and two prophecies on December 18th. All of them were given in the year 520 BC.

You can read Haggai very quickly. It is only 38 verses long.

Zechariah

I have been a fan of the 18th century evangelist, John Wesley, for a number of years. The story is told that when he was just five years old, his house caught on fire. His parents and all of the children were accounted for, except for John who was seen peering out of a second story window. The neighbors and onlookers climbed on each other's shoulders and rescued the boy just moments before the entire building collapsed. His mother remarked that he looked like a "brand plucked from the fire."

A brand is a glowing ember, like a red briquette that you might find in your barbeque pit, and that's pretty much what the little boy looked like. It was a defining moment for John Wesley who was old enough to remember the incident. For the rest of his life, he referred to himself as the "brand plucked from the fire."

When I first heard that story I assumed Susanna Wesley was simply coming up with poetic imagery, creative woman that she was. But in one of my read-throughs of Zechariah, I found the exact quote. Susanna wasn't being imaginative, she was quoting Zechariah.

Is this not a brand plucked from the fire?   *(Zechariah 3:2)*

What Bible knowledge! In a moment of extreme family crisis, Susanna had the presence of mind to recall a minor verse from a minor prophet and apply it to a desperate situation.

Now, back to the book of Zechariah. It is longest of the minor prophets in word count, and it is also one of the most challenging to understand.

Zechariah was an exact contemporary of Haggai, and like Haggai, some of the prophecies are precisely dated to the 2nd year of King Darius (520 BC). In terms of content, Zechariah is divided into two sections, the first relating to the building of the temple, and the second relating to end times. In your read through, see if you can find where the first part ends and the second begins.

Zechariah is of particular interest to eschatologists, people who study how the world will end. Along with the book of Daniel, Zechariah gives valuable information. I like the part where Jesus descends from heaven and places His foot on the Month of Olives which splits in two, from east to west. Now that will be quite a sight!

Enjoy Zechariah. Some chapters are difficult, but those relating to the end times are downright exciting!

Malachi

Malachi is the last of the twelve minor prophets, and with it the Old Testament comes to an end. If you are reading the Bible sequentially, you can give yourself a major pat on the back when you finish Malachi. You have just read the entire Old Testament. It's quite an accomplishment!

Malachi addresses the people with a series of issues that He has against them, and the people answer with innocent, "when did we do that?" types of questions. Then He levels it to them with no uncertain terms. God has significant things to say about how divorce displeases Him, and about how our failure to tithe displeases Him, and so forth.

Personally, I get pretty convicted over not tithing properly when I read Malachi. What about you? Are you thinking about getting a divorce? Read Malachi before you take that step.

There are some wonderful blessings in Malachi which will be ours when we behave ourselves properly before God. As you read, take casual notes and list these blessings as you come across them.

Malachi provides the perfect transition to the New Testament in that it closes with the promise that Elijah will return before the coming of the Messiah. The New Testament opens with the birth of Jesus Christ. Jesus' first act as an adult (before beginning his ministry at age thirty) was to be baptized by John the Baptist in the Jordan River. We believe that John the Baptist was the same Elijah that Malachi predicted.

Read Malachi with enthusiasm – and then prepare your heart for the treat you'll experience when you read the next book in the Bible, the Gospel of Matthew.

Chapter 27

Book by Book: The Gospels and Acts

If you are reading the Bible straight through from Genesis to Revelation, you have now finished the Old Testament and you're starting on the New Testament. You'll notice a significant change in tone.

The word *gospel* means "good news." By the time the gospels are written, most of the bad news prophecies in the Old Testament have come to pass. Babylon has been destroyed. Nineveh is gone. Edom, the Amalekites, Moab, the Philistines, and all the rest of Judah's enemies are gone. Egypt is no longer a threat. Even the unfaithful ten tribes of the Northern Kingdom, Israel, haven't been heard from for nearly six hundred years.

The Southern Kingdom, Judah, has survived the Babylonian captivity, and they have learned their lesson. They are no longer going after foreign gods. Historically, the time is ripe for the Messiah to come, and that is the "good news."

And the Messiah *really did come!* There are unbelievers who like to think that Jesus was a mythical character. But no, He was born, He grew up, He walked on this earth. He was a real human being with bones, muscles, lungs and a heart that pumped blood through His body until the moment He died.

His earliest followers knew Him as a real person, and as time went by, four men decided to write the story of the Lord they knew so well during His time on earth.

The Gospel of Matthew

The New Testament opens with Matthew's account of events.

Matthew was one of Jesus' twelve disciples. He was originally known as Levi, the son of Alphaeus, and was a tax collector by profession. One day, Jesus passed by the tax office, saw Levi sitting there and said, "Follow me!" And that's how life instantly changed for Levi, who was known as Matthew for the rest of his life.

Of the four gospel writers, Matthew is the most "Jewish." Matthew spends more time than any other gospel writer pointing out events in Jesus' life that fulfilled Old Testament prophecies.

Here is an example. After Jesus was born, God told Joseph in a dream to take Mary and Jesus to Egypt because King Herod wanted to kill Him. Matthew records that as soon as Joseph woke up from the dream,

> ... he took the young Child and His mother by night and departed for Egypt, and was there until the death of Herod, that it might be fulfilled which was spoken by the Lord through the prophet, saying, "Out of Egypt I called My Son."   (Matt 2:14-15)

Matthew is quoting the prophet Hosea, giving one of many examples of how events in Jesus' life prove that He is the Messiah.

Matthew was probably written sometime in the 70's. That is, 40 or so years after the death and resurrection of Christ. By this time thousands of Gentiles were coming to the Lord, people who had no concept of Old Testament prophecies. So, one of Matthew's purposes in writing his gospel is to provide a clear link between the Old Testament and Jesus the Messiah.

Here is an interesting fact about Matthew's gospel. He uses the term "kingdom of heaven" thirty-two times. The other gospels don't use the term at all. They talk about the "kingdom of God."

For example, Matthew says, "The kingdom of heaven is like leaven, which a woman took and hid in three measures of meal till it was all leavened." Luke says, "To what shall I liken the kingdom of God? It is like leaven, which a woman took and hid in three measures of meal till it was all leavened."

Clearly the concepts are the same, so why did Matthew prefer "the kingdom of heaven' over "the kingdom of God?" To be honest, I don't know, but it is something I'm mulling over these days. Scholars have their opinions, but whatever the reason, we know this: each gospel writer brings his own personality and values to the table in his presentation of the gospel. *Matthew was a kingdom of heaven kind of guy.*

As you read Matthew's gospel, learn everything you can about our Lord and Savior, Jesus Christ. But don't miss the chance to get to know Matthew as well. As you read, take note of his passions, his values, his sense of important things – and his personality, too.

The Gospel of Mark

Mark is believed to be the first of the four gospels, written in Rome most likely in the mid-60's but perhaps as early as the late 50's. This was during the oppressive reign of the Roman Emperor Nero whose persecution of Christians is legendary.

Short and sweet, the Gospel of Mark cuts to the chase. Mark's gospel has a sense of urgency about it which implies that he wanted to get the good news out as quickly as possible – before the people who knew it best got murdered.

And they did get murdered! The apostles Peter and Paul were both put to death in Rome during Nero's reign, and all the other disciples and early church leaders were killed off one by one as they carried out their ministries throughout the known world. Tradition holds that the Apostle John was the only one of Jesus' twelve disciples to die a natural death.

Mark himself was not one of the twelve, but he was a close associate of the Apostle Peter who no doubt told Mark everything he could about his time with the Lord. Some scholars consider the Gospel of Mark to be a collection of Peter's reminiscences about Jesus.

Nevertheless, Mark had his own purposes in writing his gospel. He puts forth the life of Christ with a concise clarity that is unmatched in the other gospels. He doesn't bother with preliminaries such as Jesus' birth. After a brief introduction, Mark records the baptism and temptation of Jesus, the calling of the first disciples, and the beginnings of His ministry of healing the sick, and casting out demons – all in the first chapter.

The gospel continues for a few chapters with Jesus engaging the crowds, proclaiming the good news through healings and miracles and teaching the people with parables. In time, opposition to His ministry increases, and Jesus spends less time in public ministry and more time with His disciples, teaching them privately.

Eventually, the opposition becomes so severe that Jesus is crucified. Mark spends about a third of his gospel recording the last week of Jesus' life on earth, His death and His resurrection.

Since Mark is short and concise, it is also high impact. I recommend reading Mark at one sitting if you have the time. It will take a little over an hour at average reading speed, and you'll get the ultimate high impact experience.

The Gospel of Luke

The Gospel of Luke is the longest of the four gospels in word count (although Matthew has more chapters, it has fewer words than Luke). It is also the most engaging in that Luke displays a mastery of the Greek language unmatched by the others. His words simply *flow*.

Luke was a highly educated follower of Jesus who accompanied the Apostle Paul on some of his journeys. He was with Paul on his journey to Rome, and he stayed there during Paul's imprisonment. One of Paul's prison letters, Colossians, mentions Luke and refers to him as "the beloved physician." (Colossians 4:14)

It's interesting to learn about Luke's profession. The fact that he was a physician might explain his special attention to Jesus' compassion for underprivileged people. Jesus healed the sick and raised the dead, and one afternoon he fed 5,000 hungry people. Although these stories are found in the other gospels, Luke tends to hone in on them with more detail and with more compassion.

Luke also places a lot of emphasis on the teachings of Jesus, namely His sermons and His parables. All told, Luke (because it is the longest gospel) fills out Jesus life and ministry with greater detail than the other gospels.

Luke is also the master historian among the four gospel writers. He consistently placed events in the context of secular history. Here are some examples.

And it came to pass in those days that a decree went out from Caesar Augustus that all the world should be registered. This

census first took place while Quirinius was governing Syria.
(Luke 2:1-2)

Luke goes on to say that Joseph took Mary to Bethlehem to register with the census, and that Jesus was born while they were there.

The point here is to note the historical detail which is found only in Luke. From secular history we know that Augustus was Emperor of Rome from 27 BC until his death on August 19, AD 14. We can also do historical research on when Quirinius was governor of Syria and when the census took place.

In the next chapter Luke tells about the preaching of John the Baptist and the baptism of Jesus. Again, we can use Luke's historical data to learn what year Jesus was baptized.

Now in the fifteenth year of the reign of Tiberius Caesar, Pontius Pilate being governor of Judea, Herod being tetrarch of Galilee, his brother Philip tetrarch of Iturea and the region of Trachonitis, and Lysanias tetrarch of Abilene, while Annas and Caiaphas were high priests, the word of God came to John the son of Zacharias in the wilderness. (Luke 3:1-2)

From secular history we know that Tiberius took over as Emperor of Rome when Augustus died in AD 14. Add 15 years, and we have AD 29 as the year of Jesus' baptism.

But guard yourself against getting caught up in detail when reading Luke. We are engaged in Bible reading, not Bible study at this point. We can easily get distracted by interesting things that come under the realm of "future Bible study," but if we do that, we could miss the entire point of Luke's gospel which is this:

"...for the Son of Man has come to seek and to save that which was lost." (Luke 19:10)

Interlude: a Note on the Synoptic Gospels

Before we move on to the gospel of John, I'd like to point out that the preceding gospels, Matthew, Mark and Luke, have a lot of passages in common. They are known as the *synoptic* gospels.

The word synoptic means "seen together," and if you "see them together," you'll note how similar these gospels are to one another. They trace the life of Christ with an almost identical outline, and they tell many of the same stories often with the very same words.

As noted, Mark is the shortest and most concise of the gospels. Many scholars believe Mark was the first one written, with Matthew and Luke duplicating and then expanding on stories found in Mark's gospel. Matthew and Luke also fill in a few details in Jesus' life that are missing in Mark's gospel – such as His birth in Bethlehem.

If you choose to study this topic, there is a lot of scholarly research on the synoptic gospels, their similarities and differences and how they came into being. Our purpose here is simply to point out that the next gospel, John, is very different from the first three gospels.

The Gospel of John

The book of John begins with a prologue that thrills me every time I read it. It starts off with,

In the beginning was the Word, and the Word was with God and the Word was God... (John 1:1)

The prologue is 18 verses long and it ranks with the greatest poetic forms in the entire Bible. In his prologue, John establishes beyond all doubt that Jesus Christ is God who "became flesh and dwelt among us."

Thus, from the very first words, John's gospel has a different *feel* to it than the other gospels. John's approach to telling the life of Christ has a systematic, literary component that drives the central message home – point by point throughout the gospel.

The synoptic gospels were most likely written in the 60's and 70's AD and distributed among the believers at the time. John didn't write his gospel until much later, in 90 or 95 AD.

At the time of Jesus' ministry, John was one of the twelve disciples, probably the youngest of them. He refers to himself as "the disciple whom Jesus loved." Of course, Jesus loved all of them, but had a special relationship with John. John was also part of Jesus' inner circle of just three disciples (Peter, James and John) who were with Jesus on certain occasions without the other nine.

By the time he wrote his gospel, John had become a very old

man. He had observed the development of Christianity in the first fifty years or so of its history, and he wrote his gospel in light of his unique perspective of events.

Specifically, John chose not to repeat much of the material covered in the synoptic gospels. For example, there are *no parables* in the book of John. There are also *no sermons* in John, and there are very few interactions with crowds.

John sets forth evidence of Jesus Messiahship with a series of well targeted examples. Did Jesus perform miracles? Yes, and John records seven (yes, exactly seven, not six or eight) miracles. He also records seven (exactly seven) instances where Jesus used the words "I am" to describe Himself. These are:

- I am the bread of life
- I am the light of the world
- I am the door of the sheep
- I am the good shepherd
- I am the resurrection and the life
- I am the way and the truth and the life
- I am the true vine

On the night of Jesus' arrest, He spent time eating the Passover meal with His disciples. The gospel of John devotes five chapters to this event. As soon as the meal ended Jesus washed the disciples feet. Then He gave them His final series of teachings before His death. Lastly He prayed for them. Jesus final prayer for His disciples is called the High Priestly Prayer, and it is recorded in John, chapter 17.

After that, the group went out to the Mount of Olives where Jesus was arrested, put on trial, crucified and placed in a tomb, all within the next 18 hours or so. The rest of John records His resurrection and his final days on earth before His ascension into heaven.

John sums up his reason for writing his gospel in this poignant passage:

> *And truly Jesus did many other signs in the presence of His disciples, which are not written in this book; but these are written that you may believe that Jesus is the Christ, the Son of God, and that believing you may have life in His name.*
> *(John 20:30-31)*

I believe you will appreciate the Gospel of John as much as I do. It's a book that grows on you each time you read it.

The Acts of the Apostles

Now we come to the only book of history in the New Testament. And, appropriately enough, the book of Acts was written by that master historian, Luke.

Let's go back and take a look at the opening verses of Luke's gospel.

> *Inasmuch as many have taken in hand to set in order a narrative of those things which have been fulfilled among us, just as those who from the beginning were eyewitnesses and ministers of the word delivered them to us, it seemed good to me also, having had perfect understanding of all things from the very first, to write to you an orderly account, most excellent Theophilus, that you may know the certainty of those things in which you were instructed. (Luke 1:1-3)*

Here Luke makes it clear that he is writing his gospel for the audience of one specific man, a believer named Theophilus. Luke's purpose is also clear. He wrote so that Theophilus would know "the certainty of those things in which you were instructed."

Who was Theophilus? We don't know. Bible researchers have their theories, but all of them are based on limited evidence.

Now in the opening verses of Acts, Luke says,

> *The former account I made, O Theophilus, of all that Jesus began both to do and teach, until the day in which He was taken up ... (Acts 1:1-2)*

In other words, Luke has decided to write another volume of information to give to Theophilus. This volume picks up where the first volume (the Gospel of Luke) ends, with Jesus' ascension into heaven.

After Jesus' resurrection He was seen on various occasions walking on earth and giving encouragement and instructions to His disciples. Now in the opening chapter of Acts, Jesus ascends into heaven. One moment He was giving instructions to the disciples, and the next moment His body started rising – going up and up into the sky until a cloud covered Him.

This was the last time Jesus was seen on earth, and He will not be seen again until the Day of the Lord.

And in that day His feet will stand on the Mount of Olives,
Which faces Jerusalem on the east.
And the Mount of Olives shall be split in two,
From east to west... (Zech 14:4)

All the excitement of the first chapter is intensified in the second chapter when the Holy Spirit was poured out on the believers and they all began to speak in tongues.

From there, Acts simply keeps getting better and better. Luke faithfully documents the development of the early church from the days when they met in homes until the beginnings of a world-wide movement.

A central figure in the book of Acts is the Apostle Paul whose conversion is recorded in Acts chapter 9. Paul went on three missionary journeys, all of which are chronicled by Luke, who sometimes accompanied Paul. These missionary journeys provide the historical context for understanding Paul's letters.

Acts is an easy and fun book to read. It is filled with stories that everyone loves. In all, I think the book of Acts is my favorite New Testament book.

Read Acts, and think about where it ranks on your list of personal favorites.

Chapter 28

Book by Book: Paul's Letters

In the earliest days of church history, there were no written resources to guide the new believers. Four men, Matthew, Mark, Luke and John wrote down the story of the life and ministry of Jesus Christ. We refer to these books as the *gospels*. Luke wrote an additional book called "The Acts of the Apostles" to record historical events after the resurrection of Jesus.

While these works were being written and distributed, church leaders started writing letters to one another and to various churches. These letters were neither biographical nor historical in nature, but they gave instructions and encouragement to the earliest believers. Over time these letters were accepted as Scripture. The primary letter writer was Paul.

If you study the life of Paul, you will learn that he took three missionary journeys from the early Christian headquarters in a city called Antioch to various places in what is now mostly Turkey and Greece. Paul's letters are essentially follow-up letters to the churches he founded during these three journeys. He also wrote to people he met or worked with during this time.

At the end of his life Paul took a one-way journey to Rome, and that is where the historical record of his life ends. Many historians believe Paul was executed in Rome during the reign of Emperor Nero in about 67 AD.

Next to the gospels, Paul's letters are the most beloved portions of the New Testament. All Bible readers love Paul. I once memorized the book of Philippians because it was so special to me.

All of Paul's letters contain a simple outline of salutation, main body and closing remarks.

Paul's salutations have four elements:

1. From Paul (and sometimes a co-worker)
2. To (a church or an individual)
3. Impartation of grace and peace
4. Statement of thankfulness (in most, but not all of his letters)

Here is an example of his salutation from II Thessalonians. You'll see the four elements in bold.

> *[from] Paul, Silvanus and Timothy, **to** the church of the Thessalonians in God our Father and the Lord Jesus Christ: **Grace to you and peace** from God the Father and the Lord Jesus Christ. **We are bound to thank God always** for you, brethren*
> (II Thess 1:1-3)

The main body in some of Paul's letters are divided into two sections, theological teachings and practical teachings. Romans and Ephesians are excellent examples of this division.

Finally, Paul generally ends his letters with some closing remarks. These often include greetings from Paul's friends in whatever city he is writing from.

Paul wrote thirteen letters, nine to churches and four to individuals. Here we will review them in the order that they appear in the Bible. However, this order is not the chronological order in which they were written.

Romans

Romans was written to the believers in the church at Rome. Don't lose the historical thread here. Comb through your memory of Acts. When was a church established there? Who established it? When did Paul write this letter? How old was he? Some of Paul's letters were written from a prison cell. Was this one of them?

The book of Acts gives the best clues, but you might want to look to an outside source to date this letter. In any event, mull over the circumstances Paul was dealing with when he wrote his letter to the Romans.

Romans is a classic example of the theological and practical division in Paul's letters. Chapters 1-11 are deeply theological and parts are difficult to understand. In chapter 12 Paul changes focus and talks about practical matters for the rest of the book.

When I say that the theological portions are difficult to understand, I'm not clowning around. I remember when I was doing evangelistic work in Denmark, our team had a Bible teacher who spent two weeks lecturing on the book of Romans. He skillfully taught us the first seven chapters, and then gave a brilliant analysis of Romans 8.

By the way, everybody's favorite chapter in Romans is chapter 8. Don't miss it when you get there!

I was looking forward to hearing what he had to say about Romans 9-11, but the next day he skipped to chapter 12. I knew very well why he skipped those chapters, but I couldn't resist the opportunity to tease him a little. "Why did you skip Romans 9-11?" I asked with a bit of an undisguised chuckle.

"Too controversial," he said. We both laughed, and the conversation ended there. Theologians have been debating those three chapters for most of church history.

However, as Bible readers, we are committed to reading the Bible, every word. We are not going to skip the boring parts, the unpleasant parts, the difficult parts, and we are not going to skip Romans 9-11. When you get there, try to understand what Paul is saying. Without going into extra study, listen to the Holy Spirit as you read. Ask Him for insight and a clear understanding. Read Romans several times before you read commentaries or delve into a deep study.

Most of Paul's letters end with a greeting from Paul's friends to mutual friends in the churches. Romans has the longest of Paul's greetings, nearly the entire 16th chapter. The Bible teacher mentioned above called Romans 16 the best chapter in the whole book of Romans.

Read Romans. Yes, parts are difficult, but other parts are crystal clear. Learn everything you can as you read this jewel.

I Corinthians

Paul wrote two letters to the church at Corinth. These letters are called I Corinthians and II Corinthians.

Corinth is located in modern day Greece on the west side of a tiny strip of land that separates the two sections of mainland Greece. Its sister city was Cenchrea, situated on the east side. Corinth was a major port in Bible times. Paul founded a church there in approximately 52 AD during his second missionary journey,

You'll notice as you read I Corinthians that Paul spends a lot of time admonishing the believers in Corinth for their misconduct. Corinth was a city in moral decline, and most of the new believers in Corinth were Gentiles who did not have a concept of Jewish laws and moral traditions. Paul has to explain the difference between right and wrong at a very basic level.

Unlike many of Paul's letters, I Corinthians does not contain theological teachings. Instead, Paul goes straight to Christian behavior. He addresses sexual immorality, abuse of the Lord's supper, abuse of spiritual gifts and many other issues.

Curiously, in the middle of his rebuke of the misuse of spiritual gifts, he inserts one of the most famous and beloved passages in the Bible. It's chapter 13, the beautiful chapter on love. This is an excellent Scripture portion to meditate over and memorize.

But then, it's back to the rebuke in chapter 14. Although the church at Corinth has a bad reputation among Christians of our age, I would caution you not to be too judgmental. We face many of the same problems today.

I recently heard a sermon in which the preacher was addressing one of Paul's instructions to the people in Corinth. It was one of those instructions (head covering for women) that we in the 21st century would prefer to ignore. The good pastor said we don't have to really follow this particular mandate because Paul was speaking to a corrupt church, and the rule only applied to corrupt churches.

Excuse me? Are our 21st century churches free of corruption?

My advice for reading I Corinthians is to take Paul's instructions seriously, very seriously. Look at your local church. Are there any behavior issues that Paul might object to? Are your teens (and every-body else as well) keeping themselves sexually pure?

Do your best to follow Paul's instructions in I Corinthians, even the ones you don't like so much.

II Corinthians

Poor Paul. If ever any pastor had a problem church, it was Paul and the church at Corinth. He wrote a difficult first letter, and then took a difficult trip to Corinth to further straighten things out. Now Paul is back in Ephesus, having to deal with more bad reports from Corinth.

By now most of the earlier problems have been addressed, but there were still a few members of the congregation who didn't accept Paul's leadership. They were promoting the leadership of people who didn't teach the truth.

Paul was deeply grieved, writing out of distress and anguish and with many tears. In this letter, more than any other, Paul puts his own raw emotions on display. He loves the people of Corinth so very much!

The letter is unique in that Paul, who doesn't like to boast about his accomplishments, is forced to do exactly that to defend his position as a true apostle of Christ. We learn more about his personal biography than we do in any of his other letters. We learn of beatings, floggings, shipwrecks and hunger. On the positive side we learn that he was caught up into the third heaven where he experienced "inexpressible things" that he wasn't free to talk about.

Woven into his personal defense is great teaching on forgiveness, the New Covenant, heaven and generosity.

Paul was truly an apostle's apostle, possibly the greatest servant of the Lord that the world has ever known. Read this letter and you'll understand why we can say that.

Galatians

One of the earliest problems that the early church faced was how to treat the many Gentiles (non-Jews) who were coming to the Lord. As you have discovered in your read-through of the Old Testament, God revealed Himself to the Jews and only the Jews.

When Peter visited Cornelius in Caesaria, Gentiles came to the Lord for the first time. Peter was as amazed as anyone that God's salvation extended beyond the Jewish community.

These new believers were suddenly leaving their pagan religions and worshipping the God of Abraham, Isaac and Jacob as revealed in Jesus Christ. So, were these new believers Jews? If they were, according to Jewish law, they needed to be circumcised.

Whether or not to circumcise Gentile believers was the first theological controversy of the infant church, and it was such an important issue that the earliest church leaders held a council to decide the matter. This council was held in the city of Jerusalem in about 52 AD, and it is recorded in Acts, chapter 15.

The early Christian leaders decided, correctly, that salvation came only through faith in Jesus Christ and that requiring non-Jewish believers to follow the law of Moses would be an unnecessary burden to them.

The subject came up in the churches of Galatia where Paul had been preaching. Some overzealous Jewish believers were insisting that Gentile believers be circumcised, so Paul wrote this letter to bring instruction and correction about this important issue.

As you read through Galatians, try to gain a good grasp on the difference between law and grace as it relates to salvation. This distinction lies at the core of what we as Christians believe.

Ephesians

Last Sunday in church my pastor preached on the promises of God. What a beautiful sermon about walking in God's provision moment by moment. He has promised us so many wonderful things!

That same afternoon, I read the book of Ephesians, all of it, at one sitting. Talk about promises!

The book of Ephesians is considered by many, myself included, to be his greatest letter. Unlike most of his letters, Paul is not addressing any particular issue in Ephesians. He doesn't spend any time bringing correction or clarifying misunderstood doctrines. In Ephesians, Paul simply pours out his heart about the greatness of God and the amazing work of salvation that we find in our Lord Jesus Christ.

When you read Ephesians at one sitting, you'll experience an impact of the glory of God that is like none other. God's divine revelation of Himself flows from Paul's pen onto paper in a torrent of words.

In fact, the opening blessing, (Ephesians 1:3-14) is just one long run-on sentence in the Greek. It's like the Lord was dictating so quickly that Paul didn't even get a chance to lift his pen long enough to put in a period.

Paul talks at length about how Christ has made Jews and Gentiles into one group. He is writing as a Jew to a primarily Gentile audience – and he declares that there is no longer any difference between them. Imagine what would happen in the Middle East today if Jews and Muslims could come to Christ and grasp this truth. Unity in Christ is one of the many promises found in Ephesians.

Like many of Paul's letters, Ephesians has two distinctive parts. The first half is doctrinal, explaining how and why we have been redeemed by God. In this section he sets forth Christian unity as well as God's purpose and goal for His church.

The second half is practical. Paul explains how we must live, now that we have been redeemed by the blood of Christ. He shows how parents and children and husbands and wives can glorify God in daily life. He also talks about how we can defeat the enemy by putting on the armor of God.

When you read Ephesians, try to get the full impact by reading it in one sitting. As you read, note down all the promises you come across. Ephesians will change your life when you learn to walk in the promises and instructions you find.

Philippians

Paul's letter to the Philippians is considered by some to be the most Christ centered of all his letters. Like Ephesians, Paul isn't spending a lot of time correcting people, but he does encourage people to live together in agreement and to remain loyal in the face of constant threats from the outside. Throughout the letter, Paul emphasizes the example that our Lord Jesus Christ gave us as He walked on this earth. He is our reason for living. Paul says,

For me to live is Christ, and to die is gain. (Phil 1:21)

That is one of a treasury of memory verses you'll find in Philippians. Some others are,

My God shall supply all your need according to His riches in

glory by Christ Jesus. (Phil 4:19)

and

Rejoice in the Lord always. Again, I will say rejoice.
(Phil 4:4)

As you read through Philippians, see how many of these little nuggets you can find and note them down in your memory verse log.

I've never been one for underlining things in my Bible because I'm one of those people who can't stand anything messy-looking. A good friend doesn't have my problem. The first time he read Philippians 2:5-11, he underlined parts of it with black ink. The next time, he underlined other parts with red ink. Then he double underlined the whole section with blue ink. Then he got a yellow highlighter and went to it. Of course, he had handwritten notes in the margins with lots of exclamation points.

That certainly isn't my style. Not only were his notes messy, the text was nearly unreadable by the fifth pass. Yet, all his messy notetaking is fine with me because this sort of thing is personality driven, and all of us have our own unique God-given personalities. But here's my point:

Whether you underline the passage or not, see if you share my friend's love for that passage. For myself, I believe this passage is one of the greatest descriptions of Jesus found anywhere. What do you think? Whether you underline it or not is completely up to you.

By the way, Philippians 2:5-11 is an excellent passage to memorize and meditate over frequently. It'll keep you humble.

Colossians

Now we come to Paul's beautiful letter to the believers in a town called Colossae. As always, don't lose the historical thread when you read Colossians. Where was Paul when he wrote this letter? Who delivered the letter? Is this one of Paul's prison letters? Had Paul ever been to Colossae? Who founded the church there?

You'll find the answers to all of these questions when you read through Colossians. I'll give you one answer now: Paul had most likely never been to Colossae. In this, the letter to the Colossians is unique.

All of the other letters were written to churches or individuals that Paul was intimately familiar with.

As with many of the other churches, the church as Colossae was dealing with false teaching. When Paul received this news, he immediately wrote to them. We don't know the specific issues, but in this letter, Paul shows us how he dealt with them.

First, he reminded the believers that Christ, as Creator, Redeemer, Reconciler and King of Kings, is supreme in all things. Second, he reminded them that all believers are complete in Him. These are the pre-eminent and unchallenged themes of Colossians.

Like many of Paul's letters, Colossians is divided into theological and practical sections. Now that we are complete in Christ, we need to live in a way that glorifies Him. He is on the throne, next to God, so we need to focus our thoughts and actions on heavenly things, not earthly things.

Then Paul goes through a list of earthly activities we used to indulge in. As Christians we need to put these things away. Paul also gives wonderful advice for families and other relationships.

Colossians was written at roughly the same time as Ephesians and the two letters are sometimes referred to as the "Twin Epistles."

I Thessalonians

This letter is Paul's first, written while he was in Corinth in about 52 AD. In fact, some scholars believe it is the very first written document in the entire New Testament, predating the gospels, Acts and the other letters.

The background for this letter is recorded in Acts 17 and the first few verses of Acts 18. Paul was preaching in a city called Thessalonica when severe opposition to the gospel forced him to leave after only 2 or 3 weeks. He left an infant church there, and he was worried about how well they were faring under the persecution that had driven him out of town. Paul went on to Berea, then Athens where he couldn't stand the suspense any longer. From Athens, he sent Silas and Timothy to visit the Thessalonian Church and report back to him.

Then Paul continued to Corinth where he stayed for a while, and where he finally met up with Timothy.

The report was good, and Paul immediately sat down and wrote the Thessalonians a letter thanking God for their faithfulness in the time of trouble.

Paul's letter is encouraging and uplifting. You can tell by its tone how thrilled Paul was to learn of their well-being. It's basically a friendly letter written with great joy.

In this letter, Paul lets his readers know a little secret. He tells us what will happen when the Lord returns. He will descend from heaven with a shout, the Christians who have already died will be raised from their graves and then all of us Christians who are alive will be caught up together with them in the clouds. We'll all ascend into heaven where we will be together with the Lord forever.

This event is referred to as "the rapture" and it is only mentioned in I Thessalonians. We'll all be part of rapture someday.

The last chapter of I Thessalonians gives a series of short pithy instructions, such as

- Rejoice always
- Pray without ceasing
- Be thankful in everything
- Abstain from every form of evil
  … and so forth

I Thessalonians is Paul's first letter. How well do you think he did?

II Thessalonians

Scholars believe that II Thessalonians was written shortly after the first letter. Paul is still concerned about the people in this church, and now he has apparently heard further news, and not all of it good. Paul is basically encouraged by their progress in the Lord, but he needs to address two issues.

First, some false teachers have been telling the Thessalonians that the Day of the Lord has already come. Paul patiently explains that certain things have to happen before the Lord comes. Chapter 2 has a well-developed description of the man of lawlessness who will come first. This man is assumed to be the Anti-Christ who is well described in the book of Revelation.

Second, it has come to Paul's attention that some church members are lazy, refusing to work. This is unacceptable to Paul, and he needs to bring correction.

Here again we see Paul as the loving shepherd of his cherished little flock of believers in Thessalonica.

II Thessalonians is a short book and easy to read.

I Timothy

I Timothy is the first of Paul's three "pastoral letters," the other two being II Timothy and Titus. All three letters were written late in Paul's life. By then, Timothy had replaced Paul as the pastor of the church at Ephesus, and Titus was pastoring a church on the island of Crete.

They are called pastoral letters because they were written specifically to the pastors of these two churches, not to the congregation. This is not to say that the church members couldn't or shouldn't read them, only that the content was oriented toward church leadership.

In I Timothy, Paul addresses church government for the first time. He lists two offices, bishops (or overseers) and deacons and gives Timothy instructions about their moral qualifications, which are very high.

He also teaches Timothy how to guard the church from false teaching (a constant theme with Paul), how to deal with widows in the congregation and elders and slaves.

I Timothy is like the perfect six-chapter manual for pastors. It is warmly written because Timothy was Paul's greatly loved co-worker for many years. In the end he encourages him to "Fight the good fight of faith,"

II Timothy

II Timothy was the last letter that Paul wrote before he died. From the book of Acts we know that Paul travelled to Rome to appeal to Caesar regarding the case filed against him in Jerusalem. In the last chapter of Acts we learn that Paul arrived in Rome and lived in his own house for two years, presumably awaiting trial. The story ends there, and we don't know from Scripture what happened to Paul after that.

Bible scholars and historians believe that Paul was set free for a time, then re-arrested and sentenced to death under Emperor Nero. Historians believe that Paul was beheaded in AD 67 in Rome.

Paul wrote his last letter to Timothy urging him to come to Rome quickly. He wanted desperately to see his beloved co-worker one last time before his pending execution.

But the main purpose of the letter wasn't to ask Timothy to come to Rome. He only got to that request in the last chapter. The main purpose was to encourage him to endure the road ahead and remain steadfast in the Lord in everything. This letter is a treasure trove of loving, pastoral advice to one of Paul's closest friends.

It is also a great book for Bible memory verses such as

For God has not given us a spirit of fear, but of power and of love and of a sound mind   (II Tim 1:7)

and

All Scripture is given by inspiration of God, and is profitable for doctrine, for reproof, for correction, for instruction in righteousness. (II Tim 3:16).

I found six verses to put into my memory card collection. When you read II Timothy, see how many you can find.

Titus

Again, don't lose the historical thread for this letter. Who was Titus and what was his relationship to Paul? When did Paul write this letter? Where was Paul writing from? Was he in prison? What were the major threats to the churches when Paul wrote to Titus.

The answer to several of these questions is found in the letter itself. We learn early on that Paul left Titus in Crete for a purpose which he explains. Later he asks Titus to meet him in a town called Nicopolis. Does this sound like Paul was in prison? No.

Likewise, we can figure out who Titus was by reading the rest of Paul's letters. He mentions Titus thirteen times. From these references we learn that Titus was a Greek convert and that he worked with Paul extensively as he established churches.

Paul and Titus were working together on the island of Crete when Paul decided to move on to another place. He wanted Titus to complete some unfinished business, namely to appoint elders in every town. Later he follows up by sending more details in this letter.

Accordingly, Titus is classified as one of Paul's "pastoral letters." Paul gives instructions to Titus regarding church leadership. He is to adhere to certain criteria when appointing elders in the churches. Paul actually gives him a checklist of things to look for in an elder.

Likewise, Paul has instructions for Godly living for older women, younger women, younger men, and even slaves.

As always, Paul is guarding his people against false teaching and doctrine. The content parallels Paul's instructions to Timothy.

Pretend you are a pastor named Titus when you read this letter. What would you be thinking?

Philemon

Philemon is the shortest of Paul's letters, but perhaps the most difficult for us to swallow. It deals with slavery, an abhorrent subject to all of us.

In Roman society, wealthy people owned slaves, and if a slave ran away, he could be punished by death.

So here we have a wealthy slaveowner named Philemon who had become a Christian. At some point one of his slaves, named Onesimus, ran away. We don't know whether this happened before or after Philemon became a believer.

Later, Onesimus turned up in the city of Rome, where Paul led him to the Lord. And this is where Paul's dilemma begins.

What should Paul do? He has led a run-away slave to the Lord, and moreover he knows Philemon, his slaveowner, very well. Under Roman law, Onesimus is subject to the death penalty if he doesn't return to his legal owner. To complicate things, Paul may have led both the run-away *and* his owner to the Lord. What a messy situation!

Paul choses to return Onesimus to Philemon. As you read, note Paul's reluctance. He wanted to keep Onesimus with him – but didn't want to do so without Philemon's permission. He wanted Philemon to welcome him as a brother in Christ, not as a slave.

Today, in the 21st century, we look back in sadness. We would hope that Philemon took Paul's hint and set Onesimus free – and allowed him to return to Paul according to his wish in verse 13. But of course, we don't know.

Philemon is instructive in helping us chose between unfair choices. As you read this letter, give some thought to the principles that Paul used in making his decision. Then use these principles during times when you are forced to choose between yuck and double yuck.

Chapter 29

Book by Book: The Remaining Letters and Revelation

While Paul wrote to specific individuals and churches, there is a body of letters known as the "general" epistles. Except for Hebrews, these letters are identified by the authors, not the recipients. They were written to "general" audiences meaning they were circulated among the churches to be read by anybody. Only II John and III John have specific recipients.

There are two themes that run consistently through all these letters, and both relate to problems that threatened the early church.

First was the problem of persecution. The earliest believers, both Jewish and Gentile, faced opposition from the religious establishments of the day. In many cases the persecution resulted in death either by mob rule (as in Stephen's death) or by official execution by the government. Later, in the 2nd and 3rd centuries, persecution became even more intense. These letters give specific advice and encouragement to believers who face persecution.

The second problem was false teaching. It seems that even in the first century of Christianity, false teachers were coming out of the woodwork and leading the believers astray. Now, 2,000 years later, false teachers are still leading us astray, so these letters are as relevant to us as they were to the early believers.

The earliest Christians were on their own, so to speak, because Jesus was in heaven and there were no established Scriptures. The early church leaders began writing divinely inspired letters to the church to give guidance. The general epistles uniformly warn people about staying true to what they had been taught and warning them not to be led astray. These letters give solid advice in how to recognize false teaching and many of them contain harsh words for the perpetrators of counterfeit doctrine. In time these letters were incorporated into an accepted body of Scripture.

Hebrews

Hebrews is unique among the New Testament letters in that no one knows who wrote it. There is no salutation in this letter so neither the writer nor the recipient is identified. But in the last few verses he extends personal notes to his audience, saying that he will try to visit them soon, and that he will travel with Timothy if possible.

That is just about all we know. He was clearly known by his audience, but his identity was lost by the time those early believers died out.

But his book is of monumental importance. At this point in Church History, many Gentiles had become believers, but this letter is, as the name indicates, specifically written to a Hebrew (Jewish) audience. Hebrews is saturated with references to the Old Testament which the early Jewish believers understood and cherished. If you can somehow transform yourself into a first century Messianic Jew, you'll understand this book like no one else. Imagine the impact it had on them.

One of the key words in Hebrews the word *superior*. The writer establishes that our Lord, Jesus Christ is superior to the angels, the prophets, Moses and Joshua. He is superior to the Levitical priesthood, superior in character and ministry. And the list goes on.

The book ends with an appeal to faithfulness. We must live by faith, committed to holiness as we navigate this world of persecution.

Don't miss chapter 11, one of the most famous passages in the Bible. It is the great faith chapter which recounts with intense emotion how the Old Testament giants lived by faith.

Read this book conscientiously and let it build your faith!

James

The book of James has had its share of controversy in the history of the Christian church. It wasn't until the 4th century that scholars accepted James as worthy of admission to the New Testament Canon.

In the year 397 the Council of Carthage accepted it into the list of New Testament era books and letters that were given status as divine scripture. But that didn't bring and end to the controversy. In the 16th century, Martin Luther pronounced James "an epistle of straw."

Just the same, I love the book of James and I once committed it to memory, or at least I tried.

The author of James appears to be the man whom Paul refers to as, "the Lord's brother." We know from Matthew 13:55 that Jesus had four brothers, James, Joseph, Simon and Judas. Mark (in Mark 6:3) lists Jesus' four brothers as James, Joses, Judas and Simon. Joses would be an alternate rendering of Joseph and the listed order is different.

The New Testament lists four people named James, but this James, the Lord's brother, appears to have become a prominent leader of the church in Jerusalem and the author of this letter.

Unlike the other letters, James is entirely practical in nature. There is no theological discussion or teaching, no mention of the death and resurrection of Jesus.

He gives his first piece of practical advice in the second verse of the letter by telling believers to "count it all joy" when they face trials in their faith. Testing is a good thing, he says, and he explains why in the next few verses.

He tells people to be doers of the Word and not hearers only. This is the part where we are supposed to love (really love!) our brothers, for example. He also talks about the power of that little organ in our mouths called the tongue. He points out that we can use our tongues to bless some people and curse others. Things shouldn't be this way!

James is full of practical advice and instruction. He learned a lot growing up as one of the younger brothers of our Lord, Jesus Christ. Read this book carefully, and you'll learn a lot, too!

I Peter

One of the things I enjoy about reading Peter's letters is observing Peter himself. Yes, he is the same Peter, that impetuous disciple of our Lord. If you are familiar with the four personality types set forth by Tim LaHaye, Peter is the classic Sanguine, always acting and speaking before he thinks. Peter is the one who jumped out of the boat to follow

Jesus during the storm while the others stayed put. He is the one who refused to let Jesus wash his feet while the others willingly complied – but had a sudden change of heart and demanded that the Lord wash, "not only my feet but my head and hands also!" Peter is the one who said he would never deny Christ, then immediately denied Him three times.

After Jesus sent the Holy Spirit in Acts Chapter 2, Peter was the first disciple to jump into action. He preached the very first Christian evangelical sermon – and he led 3,000 people to the Lord that morning. As we read through the book of Acts, we watch Peter develop into a disciplined, mature, and a very effective leader of the early church. The reckless immaturity of his earlier years is gone forever.

And now we come to his first letter. Unlike the book of James, this letter was accepted immediately by the earliest believers. They loved Peter the person, and they loved his letters.

His first letter is so loving, so encouraging. He gives practical tender advice for husbands and wives and he reminds us to be holy because God is holy. He tells us to be like newborn babies, craving spiritual milk so that we can grow up properly.

He talks about living for God while simultaneously suffering for Him. We do that in part by being clear minded and self-controlled, and by loving one another with a pure heart fervently.

Read I Peter with great respect and awe. You'll come away with a heightened perception of both the man Peter and the magnitude of his message.

II Peter

Peter's first letter was immediately and universally accepted by the early church. No so with his second letter. For various reasons, scholars through the ages have wondered whether Peter was actually the author of his second letter.

Personally, I think this debate is pointless because, in the very first verse, Peter identifies himself as an apostle of Christ. Moreover, he tells us that he was with Christ on the mountain when He was transfigured. How could anyone lie about these things – and then turn around and set forth the tremendous truth found in this letter? So, I accept Peter, the apostle and early church leader, as the writer of this book.

Peter starts out with the most encouraging instructions for us about how to grow in the Lord and make our calling and election sure. Then, in chapter 2 he shifts his attention to false teachers and sets forth the strongest rebuke found anywhere in the New Testament. Peter absolutely rails against them and minces no words about their upcoming destruction.

He also talks about the eventual destruction of the earth. In Noah's day, God destroyed the earth by water, but in II Peter we learn that He will destroy it by fire next time. It is not difficult to imagine this happening today with our nuclear bombs and weapons of mass destruction.

Read II Peter. You'll like it – and you'll get some good advice for living the Christian life.

I John

I John is one of my favorite books because John addresses us as "my little children," which gives me a warm, fuzzy feeling. John, the youngest of the twelve disciples, was very old by the time he wrote this letter, and when I read it, I imagine myself a six-year-old child sitting in his grandfatherly lap listening contentedly while he tells me wonderful things about love.

And John understood the love of Christ at a deeper level than the other disciples. In his gospel, he refers to himself as "the disciple whom Jesus loved" no less than five times. On one of these occasions, he was lying next to Jesus, and he leaned onto his chest to ask Him a question.

Love is the main theme in I John. When we love God we keep His commandments. When we don't love God, we don't keep his commandments. It's pretty simple. Which kind of person am I?

As with the other letter writers, John concerns himself with false teachers and prophets (he calls them "antichrists" in this letter). How do we distinguish them? By whether or not they keep His commandments. The person who claims to know Christ but doesn't keep His commandments,

> is a liar, and the truth is not in him. But whoever keeps His Word, truly the love of God is perfected in him. (I John 2:4-5)

I John challenges me to assess my level of love for God and for people. Am I following God's commandments? If not, I don't truly love Him. Do I hate my brother? Then I am walking in darkness and not in light.

But John doesn't leave room for discouragement when we see our failures. No, there is always a way out. Here is the most famous verse in I John.

> *If we confess our sins, He is faithful and just to forgive us our sins and to cleanse us from all unrighteousness. (I John 1:9)*

Read I John with anticipation. It's the most intimate and most encouraging of the general epistles, and you'll love it.

The Final Letters

Now we come to the shortest books in the entire Bible, 2nd and 3rd John. Along with Jude, these are books that people seldom get to unless they are reading the Bible systematically. These books are so short, so close to the end of the Bible and so easily overlooked.

We won't overlook them here. Our job is to read the Bible, all of it, even the little books.

> *With God's help, I will read my Bible,*
> *every word, in the proportion that God gave,*
> *over and over again, for the rest of my life.*

II John

John the disciple of Christ wrote this letter kind of as a reinforcement of the message in I John. That is, he covers the same topics, but in a very short format.

He was writing to the "elect lady" and her children. Some people want to think this lady is a figure of a first century woman church leader (or some such thing), and her children are spiritual children in the Lord.

I have very little patience with this sort of reasoning. No, she was a real lady (possibly a widow) who had real children. Moreover, John wants to talk with her face to face when he sees her. How many times have you talked "face to face" with a figurative person?

John has a two-fold message, to continue walking in love and to reject false teachers. Again he stresses that following God's command-ments is an act of love.

> *This is love, that we walk according to His commandments.*
> *(verse 6)*

With regard to false teachers, he tells her not to even greet them or invite them into her home.

It's a short letter, only 13 verses, but don't overlook it in your reading of the Scriptures.

III John

Unlike the other general epistles, III John addresses a specific individual (a believer named Gaius) with instructions about a specific problem.

John commends Gaius for his hospitality toward travelling pas-tors and evangelists. But there was a certain church member, named Diotrephes, who liked to throw his weight around. He wouldn't receive visitors and spoke maliciously about John and the other leaders. John sternly warns Gaius against him.

Where is Diotrephes today? Totally lost to history, but John the Apostle retains monumental status as an early church leader.

In the opening salutation John makes a statement that has fasci-nated wealth seekers today. He says,

> *Beloved, I pray that you may prosper in all things and be in*
> *health, just as your soul prospers. (verse 2)*

This is the foundation verse for the so-called prosperity gospel that gained prominence in certain Christian circles in the 1980's. They interpreted prosperity as monetary wealth.

What do you think? Prosperity could refer to monetary wealth, but it could also refer to a general state of well-being as many believe.

Give these matters some thought as you read III John.

Jude

Jude, another of the books that is easily overlooked, has a message that everyone needs to hear. His main thrust is dealing with false teachers.

There is some discussion as to the identity of Jude. He says in the opening verse that he is the brother of James. We know that our Lord had four younger brothers, James, Joseph, Simon and Judas. Many believe that the writer of Jude, the brother of James, is the Judas mentioned here. If that is true, then two of our Lord's brothers wrote letters for us to read.

The book of Jude is a hard-hitting denunciation of false teachers who creep into our churches and trade God's grace for a license to immorality.

For example, Jude specifically mentions sexual immoraltiy in verse 7, As we have seen throughout the Scriptures, God utterly despises sexual immorality which He defines as any sexual activity outside of holy matrimony between a man and a woman. Yet there are false teachers, even today, who led people to believe that premarital sex, extramarital sex, homosexuality, incest and sex with animals are okay. In truth, God hates it all and calls us to account.

You can read Jude and learn what God has in store for both the false teachers and the wayward believers who fall into their trap. Jude has a forceful message that is as relevant for us today as it has ever been in history.

But from verse 20 to the end, Jude shifts his tone and encourages us to walk with the Lord during times of deception. He assures us that God is able to keep us from falling.

Revelation

Revelation is the main book (supplemented by Daniel and Zechariah and passages from a few other books) that spells out the end times. People interested in eschatology, the study of the end times, love Revelation and devote hours, days, years and decades to understanding it.

And that's what it takes: years and years to study revelation. But we aren't doing that here. We are reading Revelation and gaining an understanding of its basic message. So here's a simple overview.

The first three chapters contain messages to seven churches. These cities still exist in western Turkey, and you can visit them today.

This section of Revelation has little bearing on the study of end times.

Chapter four reveals a magnificent description of the throne room of heaven and the One sits on the throne. We'll all see the marvelous scene in person when we get there.

With chapter five, we see the beginning of the eschatological portion of the book of Revelation. There is a scroll with seven seals that no one can open. Then the lamb who was slain (that is, Jesus) is found worthy. The next several chapters describe what happens when the scroll with its seals are opened, one at a time. This is the section of Revelation that fascinates end-times enthusiasts.

The last two chapters of Revelation are the best ever. They describe the New Jerusalem and the final coming of the Lord, when God will wipe away all the tears from our eyes.

Revelation isn't the frightening book that I once thought it was. It is a truly encouraging book that tells us how everything we've read in the Bible comes together in one glorious future for all of God's children.

Congratulations!

When you've finished Revelation, you've read the whole Bible! This is a big day. You're now a Bible reading champion!

But of course, it's not the end of your Bible reading journey. Here's the Bible Reading Creed for one last time.

With God's help, I will read my Bible,
every word, in the proportion that God gave,
over and over again for the rest of my life.

We've read the Bible, every word, in the proportion that God gave. Now, we will proceed to the part about reading the Bible over and over again for the rest of our lives.

Have fun! Read, read, read! Learn, learn, learn!